June 8

Pastor [illegible]

Thank You For All You
Have Done For Our Church,
Community and Our Family
This Past 10 Years
In Christ

John Randy Eckman

Tilling God's Land

Tilling God's Land

100 Devotions for Christian Farmers

by Scott Skelly

Dedicated to the memory of Uncle Bill.

I don't know if you and I ever had a one-on-one discussion about our faith, but I only realized after you were gone that the only time you weren't willing to help on the farm was when it was time to go to church.

Introduction

"If a farmer from Old Testament times could have visited an American farm in year 1900, he would have recognized—and had the skill to use—most of the tools he saw: the hoe, the plow, the harrow, the rake. If he were to visit an American farm today, he might think he was on a different planet."

—Don and Philip Paarlberg,
The Agricultural Revolution of the 20th Century

AS A YOUNG CHILD attending St. Paul's School in Janesville, Wisconsin, I always became excited when we studied Bible stories that involved farming. My siblings and I were the only farm kids in the school, so I felt somewhat special when we talked about farming. My teachers boosted that feeling by sometimes asking me to verify some farming facts as we studied these Bible stories. Looking back, it seems ironic that I was asked to substantiate farming knowledge such as the foolishness of sheep. My father did not raise sheep, and as a second grader I had probably never even touched a sheep. Yet I went along with it all the same. I soon came to learn that the Bible involved many stories of raising crops, tending animals, and being a farmer.

Today I still sit in church and think about my own farming experiences when the pastor describes farming practices to the members to help a parable make more sense. In the twenty-first century, most churchgoers do not know a whole lot about farming. They may not readily understand some farming comparisons that God uses. As a farmer, though, I feel a sense of connection when God uses these stories to share his message. Just as every Christian can better connect to God because he came to earth as a man through Jesus, I felt a little extra connection to God when I read about farming in the Bible.

Jesus might have been the son of a carpenter, but he only talked about buildings and construction a handful of times. Farming, on the other hand, appears in many of his stories and parables, and it also appears throughout the Old and New Testaments. The Bible describes Jesus as a shepherd and shares the concern of people in times of drought. Parables talk about sowing and growing crops, and disgruntled farm laborers are compared to sinners. Sheep, rain, seeds, and soil feature prominently throughout the Bible. The first man that God created was given the task of farming. A farmer was tasked as God's agent to save creation from a flood by building an ark. The savior of the universe was even born in a barn.

Unfortunately, the world is full of sin and agriculture is often portrayed in a negative light as well. One farmer was greedy with his harvest and it cost him his life. The world's first agronomist killed his brother because he was jealous. Plagues destroyed the crops of Egypt. When we look at our farms today, we know that life is not always easy. Evil surrounds us, and Christians who are farmers face just as many struggles as those who don't farm.

Farming has changed over the past ten thousand years, yet we can still relate and feel the struggles, pain, and success that the farmers of the Bible experienced. Jesus did not talk about GPS-guided tractors in his parables, but he did talk about herdsmen and planting crops. Gloating about the role of farming in God's word as I did as a child might not be wise, but farmers do have an opportunity to make a special connection to what God is teaching us. We also know that God uses his entire word to speak to us about our daily lives, and as farmers there is definitely an ongoing need for God's support in our agricultural successes and struggles.

I have at times thought how hard it must feel to be a non-Christian farmer. Farming requires so much trust that God will provide good weather, markets, and conditions. I can do everything right in raising my crops until the day of harvest, but a single storm can destroy all my work. I need to trust that God will provide a harvest, and when my harvest is meager I need to trust that God will continue to watch over me during tough times.

As you journey through this book, you will encounter a hundred devotions relating to your role as a farmer. Some will look directly at stories of farming in the Bible. Reflect on the challenges and successes of these farmers, and consider how God works in your life with similar situations. Other devotions are specifically written to support you in your work as a farmer. A farmer will go through many tough days, but God is always there for support. He also sends us good days, and we need to be thankful for our blessings. As you read these devotions, reflect on how you can better include God in your daily work and life.

May God bless you, your family, and your farm each and every day. Thanks be to God for all that he provides.

A Party for the Cows

Luke 15:4–7

⁴Suppose one of you has a hundred sheep and loses one of them. Does he not leave the ninety-nine in the open country and go after the lost sheep until he finds it? ⁵And when he finds it, he joyfully puts it on his shoulders ⁶and goes home. Then he calls his friends and neighbors together and says, "Rejoice with me; I have found my lost sheep." ⁷I tell you that in the same way there will be more rejoicing in heaven over one sinner who repents than over ninety-nine righteous persons who do not need to repent.

I HAVE NEVER TENDED sheep, but I remember plenty of times while growing up when the dairy cattle on our farm would escape. Most would not go far, but it always seemed that one would take off and make it about half a mile. For a farmer, a lost animal is a huge deal. I was recently walking through a rural high school when a student answered her cell phone. A teacher approached the student to take away her phone, but she quickly grabbed her coat and ran away yelling, "Sorry, I have a cow standing in the middle of the road!" Smiling, the teacher waived the no-cell-phone rule and let the student go.

I can remember numerous times as a child when we would help the neighbors or they would help us when an animal got out. Suddenly, getting that animal home safely became the most important job for our neighborhood. Sometimes this required people to delay chores or lose sleep, but everyone would jump right in without hesitation.

When believers leave the fold, God wants them back, just as a farmer wants his or her animal back. Sometimes God uses those who are strong in faith to help corral that believer back to faith. We never hosted any parties when our animals were all returned home; we were just mad that the animal broke the fence in the first place. However, God is more forgiving, and he *does* celebrate when his people come back home.

11

Does that mean that we should intentionally fall away from God so that we can later come back to be welcomed joyfully by him? Of course not! I doubt any farmer would care for an animal more after catching it than if the animal had never run away at all. Lucky for us, God is not like this. God really wants us to be a part of his kingdom. He wants every human to be with him one day in heaven. Every day he rejoices over those who believe in him. When someone falls away, it causes him a lot of pain. So when someone comes back to him, he rejoices in having that believer with him. The bottom line is that God wants all people to believe so that they can join him in heaven one day.

Storms on the Farm

Matthew 14:22–32

[22]Immediately Jesus made the disciples get into the boat and go on ahead of him to the other side, while he dismissed the crowd. [23]After he had dismissed them, he went up on a mountainside by himself to pray. Later that night, he was there alone, [24]and the boat was already a considerable distance from land, buffeted by the waves because the wind was against it.

[25]Shortly before dawn Jesus went out to them, walking on the lake. [26]When the disciples saw him walking on the lake, they were terrified. "It's a ghost," they said, and cried out in fear.

[27]But Jesus immediately said to them: "Take courage! It is I. Don't be afraid." [28]"Lord, if it's you," Peter replied, "tell me to come to you on the water." [29]"Come," he said. Then Peter got down out of the boat, walked on the water and came toward Jesus. [30]But when he saw the wind, he was afraid and, beginning to sink, cried out, "Lord, save me!"

[31]Immediately Jesus reached out his hand and caught him. "You of little faith," he said, "why did you doubt?" [32]And when they climbed into the boat, the wind died down.

A STORM RECENTLY passed through our area that brought winds in excess of fifty miles per hour for a few days. The meteorologists were all excited that it was the storm of the decade, but to me it just seemed like another really windy few days. However, since it was late October it wreaked havoc on the corn crop.

We were certainly thankful that we had most of our crops in, and the storm did not cause any major structural damages. However, I was frustrated, because combining would be much more difficult for our few remaining acres. As I often find myself doing, I began to ask God why he was sending such bad weather to our farm and making it so difficult for us. It seems that the weather never cooperates. It feels as if we are always in a drought or getting flooded; that the weather is cold so nothing grows or the heat is scorching the plants.

As farmers, it is easy to be depressed about the weather. This is why we need to trust that God is in control. When the weather is not going our way, prayer is certainly a good thing. But it can be frustrating when, after we call out to God, the weather does not change.

In Matthew 14, we see the disciples battling in a storm of their own. They too were very afraid, and even at a time when they needed to trust Jesus, they did not recognize him. Only when Jesus asked Peter to trust in him did the recognition take place. However, even when he was out of the boat coming to Jesus on the water, the storm did not pass for Peter. His faith was still being tested.

We are going to have storms of our own in life, whether they are physical storms or other problems. Just because we ask God to take them away does not mean that they will immediately be gone. However, even when we are experiencing bad times, God is beside us. The problem might not disappear, but he will stand by our side if we allow him to.

The Seed and the Planter

Matthew 13:3–9, 18–23

[3]Then he told them many things in parables, saying: "A farmer went out to sow his seed. [4]As he was scattering the seed, some fell along the path, and the birds came and ate it up. [5]Some fell on rocky places, where it did not have much soil. It sprang up quickly, because the soil was shallow. [6]But when the sun came up, the plants were scorched, and they withered because they had no root. [7]Other seed fell among thorns, which grew up and choked the plants. [8]Still other seed fell on good soil, where it produced a crop—a hundred, sixty or thirty times what was sown. [9]He who has ears, let him hear."

[18]"Listen then to what the parable of the sower means: [19]When anyone hears the message about the kingdom and does not understand it, the evil one comes and snatches away what was sown in his heart. This is the seed sown along the path. [20]The one who received the seed that fell on rocky places is the man who hears the word and at once receives it with joy. [21]But since he has no root, he lasts only a short time. When trouble or persecution comes because of the word, he quickly falls away. [22]The one who received the seed that fell among the thorns is the man who hears the word, but the worries of this life and the deceitfulness of wealth choke it, making it unfruitful. [23]But the one who received the seed that fell on good soil is the man who hears the word and understands it. He produces a crop, yielding a hundred, sixty or thirty times what was sown."

JESUS TELLS HIS DISCIPLES a parable about a farmer sowing seeds in a field. It is interesting that the farmer in the parable faces some of the same challenges we face today. Let's imagine that Jesus was telling this parable today:

A farmer went out with his John Deere corn planter to plant his cornfield. As he was planting the seed, some fell on the lane when he turned around at the end of the field, and the birds came and ate it up. Parts of his field had rocky, clumpy, or sandy soil. In those places, seed sprang up quickly because the soil was shallow and warm. But when the sun came up, the corn plants were scorched, and they withered because they had no roots. Other seed was planted in a patch of thistles that the farmer could never seem to eliminate. The thistles grew up and choked the plants. Still other seed was planted in good soil, where it produced a crop—two hundred bushels to the acre, which was many times more than what was sown.

It certainly is interesting how the parable of the sower is so familiar to us today. But like all parables in the Bible, it is not the story but the meaning that holds value. Verses 18–23 explain the parable:

Seed that falls on the lane cannot grow because it has no soil base to even begin growth. Think of how many people you know who have heard Bible stories, but do not really understand Christianity. You may know others whose seed fell in shallow or sandy soil. Like these seeds, the faith grows fast, but with no base or constant support, it quickly dries up and dies. We have also seen people, or even ourselves, get choked out by the evil of this world. We can see that the thistles and evil around us are wrong, but we continue to live right in the middle of them.

Yet, when we choose the good soil of a life lived for God, we grow exponentially. We continue to grow as time goes on. If we continue to live in Christ throughout our lives, our corn plant will continue to grow until the day our farmer, Jesus, takes us to heaven. Judgment Day will be the ultimate harvest. Is your corn plant growing in the right soil?

Your Insurance Policy

Psalm 33:16–19

[16]No king is saved by the size of his army;
no warrior escapes by his great strength.
[17]A horse is a vain hope for deliverance;
despite all its great strength it cannot save.
[18]But the eyes of the LORD are on those who fear him,
on those whose hope is in his unfailing love,
[19]to deliver them from death
and keep them alive in famine.

WHAT'S YOUR EXIT STRATEGY? Do you plan for a way to turn back when things do not go as planned? What do you do when you start losing the battles of life?

For an army going into battle, the soldiers need to plan a way to get out in case everything goes wrong. Verse 17 says: "A horse is a vain hope for deliverance; despite all its great strength it cannot save." A soldier might rely on a horse to get him out, but that horse may fail. It could fall, get injured, or run away in the heat of a battle. Even if that horse was the best horse in the kingdom, it becomes worthless to the soldier.

As farmers, what is our strategy when things go wrong? If you hedge crop prices, you try to put protection in place in case the prices fall. Or maybe you own crop insurance in case your crop dies from drought, insects, or another disaster. Farmers have many ways to help buy or insure security, at least to some degree, for their farms and families. While farmers know that they may still have uncertain times, they also know that the protection they receive will help to compensate for the loss. However, though we may spend lots of time tracking the security of our farm to provide for our families, are we also spending the time to ensure our eternal security?

As Christians, we also have that built-in security. Unlike crop markets, our promise of security is certain and for eternity. While God tells us that his answer will not always be yes to a bountiful earthly harvest, we have the eternal promise of heaven that will always be yes if we believe in Christ. In him we can have the best security of all.

Surely such great protection must come at a high premium. But no . . . the premium has already been paid! The ultimate security is a free gift from Christ. We cannot *earn* eternal life. We simply need to believe that Jesus died to forgive our sins if we ask for forgiveness. This is good for us, because otherwise we would surely not be able to afford this insurance. Plus, when we have a relationship with Jesus, he is also a resource to help us handle those daily challenges of life here on earth. Thank the Lord for such a wonderful gift!

Can Man Play God?

Genesis 1:24–31

²⁴And God said, "Let the land produce living creatures according to their kinds: livestock, creatures that move along the ground, and wild animals, each according to its kind." And it was so. ²⁵God made the wild animals according to their kinds, the livestock according to their kinds, and all the creatures that move along the ground according to their kinds. And God saw that it was good.

²⁶Then God said, "Let us make man in our image, in our likeness, and let them rule over the fish of the sea and the birds of the air, over the livestock, over all the earth, and over all the creatures that move along the ground."

²⁷So God created man in his own image,

    in the image of God he created him;

    male and female he created them.

²⁸God blessed them and said to them, "Be fruitful and increase in number; fill the earth and subdue it. Rule over the fish of the sea and the birds of the air and over every living creature that moves on the ground."

²⁹Then God said, "I give you every seed-bearing plant on the face of the whole earth and every tree that has fruit with seed in it. They will be yours for food.

³⁰And to all the beasts of the earth and all the birds of the air and all the creatures that move on the ground—everything that has the breath of life in it—I give every green plant for food." And it was so.

³¹God saw all that he had made, and it was very good. And there was evening, and there was morning—the sixth day.

IT IS SOMETIMES EASY to forget about God's power in our lives. As a livestock owner in the twenty-first century, it can be pretty easy to forget that God is the maker and caretaker of all animals. With practices such as selective breeding and artificial insemination, it becomes easy to think that humans are in control of making animals. Look at what livestock looked like a hundred years ago, and see how humans have improved this. We have larger, stronger, and healthier livestock than ever before. In fact, a side-by-side comparison of modern livestock with livestock of the past would show a stark difference in size and shape.

Crop farmers can see changes too. According to the Corn Farmers Coalition, farmers grow five times more corn on twenty percent less land today than they did in the 1930s. Surely humans must really be in control if we can make such great advances.

Genesis 1 puts things back into perspective. God created the world out of nothing. He did not start with a poorly performing cow and breed selective traits. He probably said something like, "Let there be a cow here and let it have life, blood, bones, the ability to reproduce, and even the characteristics that will allow humans to alter it with time as their need arises." He created everything from nothing. While scientists all over the world try to convince us that the complex workings of an animal, in addition to the rest of the earth's living things, evolved from a simple spark in a broth of elements, I find believing in God to be a more logical choice.

Despite all our advances in science, God still sends us simple reminders of his power. Our animals still suffer from sickness, and our crops still die from drought and flood. Even our advances get squashed sometimes. Diseases build up resistance to drugs, and chemicals seem to not do their jobs after a while. These are all gentle reminders of God's control.

The God who created this universe also created humans, who will slowly learn to improve his creation for their own benefit. God still rules the universe, but he gives us the gift of a little power from time to time. When we study and learn about his creation, we learn about ways that God left for us to use our abilities to release new traits and techniques that he has known about all along. It is our job to remember that God gave us that power and knowledge to unlock his creation.

Farming Next to Jesus

Colossians 3:15–17, 23–24

¹Let the peace of Christ rule in your hearts, since as members of one body you were called to peace. And be thankful. ¹⁶Let the message of Christ dwell among you richly as you teach and admonish one another with all wisdom through psalms, hymns, and songs from the Spirit, singing to God with gratitude in your hearts. ¹⁷And whatever you do, whether in word or deed, do it all in the name of the Lord Jesus, giving thanks to God the Father through him.

²³Whatever you do, work at it with all your heart, as working for the Lord, not for human masters, ²⁴since you know that you will receive an inheritance from the Lord as a reward. It is the Lord Christ you are serving.

WHEN I WAS LITTLE, a teacher told our class that God had a special plan for each of us. She told us that God would do something special with our lives. For the next few weeks, I wondered what that special thing would be. How was I going to know when the special thing happened? Did this mean that my entire class would become ministers and church leaders?

Today, I think I have a better understanding of what my teacher was talking about. Colossians 3:17 explains: "And whatever you do, whether in word or deed, do it all in the name of the Lord Jesus, giving thanks to God the Father through him." So does this mean that every time I plant my crops, feed the livestock, or go about my daily farming tasks I am doing it in the name of the Lord? Yes it does!

Doing our tasks serves the Lord in two ways. First, your occupation is vital to society, and everyone has a different task. If everyone in my class had become ministers, who would be the farmers, police officers, and garbage collectors? While every occupation holds its own importance to society, as farmers we can see a definite need for our work. We produce many of the base products that feed, fuel, and clothe our nation and the world. Without farmers, society could not function. Even Jesus needed farmers so that he could eat while he was ministering. (Certainly, he did feed thousands of people with a small basket of bread and fish, but most of the time he relied on farmers and fishermen.) So simply doing our work fulfills the daily needs of God's people. By doing this, we serve the Lord.

However, you do not need to be a Christian to help supply the needs of humanity. So what sets Christian farmers apart? Verses 15 and 16 stress the need to be thankful to God and surround ourselves with the message of God. When you bring in a successful crop, do you offer the Lord a prayer of thanks? When a crop gets destroyed by weather, do you thank God for sparing your family and buildings? To whom do you credit the success of your farm? God sends us the rain and the sun. He allows our cows to produce milk, and our pigs to put on weight. Do you give thanks to God, or do you just accept these occurrences as acts of nature?

The second way our work serves the Lord is in the way we perform our daily tasks. Are you honest with your buyers and providers? When a cow steps on your foot, what words come out of your mouth? What types of rumors do you spread about your neighbors? We all slip up from time to time because of our human nature. But think about how you might act differently if you had Jesus working beside you in the barn.

Our earthly tasks are important to God and to those around us. God tells us that when we perform those tasks to glorify him, our reward will not be on earth but in heaven. Are you farming for the Lord?

Uncompensated Work

Luke 15:11–32 (NKJV)

[11]Then He said: "A certain man had two sons. [12]And the younger of them said to his father, 'Father, give me the portion of goods that falls to me.' So he divided to them his livelihood. [13]And not many days after, the younger son gathered all together, journeyed to a far country, and there wasted his possessions with prodigal living. [14]But when he had spent all, there arose a severe famine in that land, and he began to be in want. [15]Then he went and joined himself to a citizen of that country, and he sent him into his fields to feed swine. [16]And he would gladly have filled his stomach with the pods that the swine ate, and no one gave him anything.

[17]"But when he came to himself, he said, 'How many of my father's hired servants have bread enough and to spare, and I perish with hunger! [18]I will arise and go to my father, and will say to him, "Father, I have sinned against heaven and before you, [19]and I am no longer worthy to be called your son. Make me like one of your hired servants."'

[20]"And he arose and came to his father. But when he was still a great way off, his father saw him and had compassion, and ran and fell on his neck and kissed him. [21]And the son said to him, 'Father, I have sinned against heaven and in your sight, and am no longer worthy to be called your son.'

[22]"But the father said to his servants, 'Bring out the best robe and put it on him, and put a ring on his hand and sandals on his feet. [23]And bring the fatted calf here and kill it, and let us eat and be merry; [24]for this my son was dead and is alive again; he was lost and is found.' And they began to be merry.

[25]"Now his older son was in the field. And as he came and drew near to the house, he heard music and dancing. [26]So he called one of the servants and asked what these things meant. [27]And he said to him, 'Your brother has come, and because he has received him safe and sound, your father has killed the fatted calf.'

[28]"But he was angry and would not go in. Therefore his father came out and pleaded with him. [29]So he answered and said to his father, 'Lo, these many years I have been serving you; I never transgressed your commandment at any time; and yet you never gave me a young goat, that I might make merry with my friends. [30]But as soon as this son of yours came, who has devoured your livelihood with harlots, you killed the fatted calf for him.'

[31]"And he said to him, 'Son, you are always with me, and all that I have is yours. [32]It was right that we should make merry and be glad, for your brother was dead and is alive again, and was lost and is found.'"

THE GOOD GUY SURE got the raw deal in the parable of the prodigal son. Look at all the hard work he had done for so many years on his father's farm. He had probably spent endless days working in the fields, and he certainly had dealt with more than his share of stubborn animals. He had been working his tail off for years and barely received even a thank you from his father.

The older son probably could have handled this if it were not for his evil brother. That creep took half the family wealth and ran away. While brother number one was working hard, brother number two was not even lifting a finger. He was flat-out lazy! Then he had the nerve to come running home to papa, who ended up throwing him a welcome-home party!

God wants all of his children in heaven, even if they have done some really bad things. He is always open to offer forgiveness and give us another chance. Verse 31 gives another message, although it is often missed by readers of this parable: " 'My son,' the father said, 'you are always with me, and all that I have is yours.'" The father told his son that payment for his labor had not yet begun. He would receive his reward, but he would have to wait. While he received the daily benefits of his labor, such as food and shelter, the greatest reward was yet to come.

As Christians, we are waiting for our great reward too: our place in heaven. As farmers, we sometimes feel like the older son. We work hard at our job, but when the books get balanced, the reward seems very small. Sometimes that reward is so small that it puts extra stress on our family simply to survive. But, though our earthly reward is sometimes small, we know that our reward in heaven will be great regardless of our financial or physical success as a farmer on earth. Our faith and repentance on earth are what will take us to heaven through the gift of God's grace. Certainly we do not earn our way to heaven, but in a sense the true reward is yet to come.

By the way: if you have kids helping with your farm, remember to reward them from time to time. They might not ask for a fattened calf or young goat, but even a simple thank you can go a long way!

A Time for Everything

Ecclesiastes 3:1–8

¹ There is a time for everything,
 and a season for every activity under the heavens:
² a time to be born and a time to die,
 a time to plant and a time to uproot,
³ a time to kill and a time to heal,
 a time to tear down and a time to build,
⁴ a time to weep and a time to laugh,
 a time to mourn and a time to dance,
⁵ a time to scatter stones and a time to gather them,
 a time to embrace and a time to refrain from embracing,
⁶ a time to search and a time to give up,
 a time to keep and a time to throw away,
⁷ a time to tear and a time to mend,
 a time to be silent and a time to speak,
⁸ a time to love and a time to hate,
 a time for war and a time for peace.

THANK GOD FOR THE SEASONS! As I write this, our farm is wrapping up another season. Most of the field work has been completed for the fall, and the machinery is getting packed tightly in the shed for the winter. I find that many people here in Wisconsin do not like winter because of all the cold and snow. While I do not enjoy either much, I do like the change of season because it gives me a chance to catch up, take a breath, and do a few new jobs such as plowing snow for a few months. By March I will be ready for the season to change again, but for now I am happy.

I think God created the seasons with farmers in mind. It gives us a break, or at least a change of pace. It keeps our jobs fresh. Winter can be a challenge for any farmer dealing with broken water pipes and frozen manure spreaders, but at least there are no flies. As spring comes around we get excited for a new season to start. Summer brings warm days with plenty of work. By fall we are glad for a break from the heat as our last big push for the year kicks in before we are back to winter.

Just like the seasons farmers experience, Ecclesiastes talks about seasons or times for other things. God has complete control of some of these, such as birth and death. Other times he lets us decide when to speak or be silent. This is one of the freedoms we have as children of God. While God is in control, we are not pawns. He does not control our every move. He lets us decide when the right time is for many of the things we do.

God also tells us that things will not always be perfect in our seasons of life. There are times when we will weep, and there are times when we will mourn. But he also promises that there will be times to laugh and times to dance. God tells us that there will be bad times in our lives. Things will not always be perfect. But he also promises good times. The bad days will eventually pass.

The next time life has you down, remember that better days will come. While God may give us freedom that results in pain, he also promises to never give us more than we can bear. When tough times have you down, remember the words of a little blue fish from the children's movie *Finding Nemo*: "Just keep swimming, just keep swimming, just keep swimming, swimming, swimming, swimming."

God Sightings

Genesis 41:17–32

[17]Then Pharaoh said to Joseph, "In my dream I was standing on the bank of the Nile, [18]when out of the river there came up seven cows, fat and sleek, and they grazed among the reeds. [19]After them, seven other cows came up—scrawny and very ugly and lean. I had never seen such ugly cows in all the land of Egypt. [20]The lean, ugly cows ate up the seven fat cows that came up first. [21]But even after they ate them, no one could tell that they had done so; they looked just as ugly as before. Then I woke up.

[22]"In my dreams I also saw seven heads of grain, full and good, growing on a single stalk. [23]After them, seven other heads sprouted—withered and thin and scorched by the east wind. [24]The thin heads of grain swallowed up the seven good heads. I told this to the magicians, but none could explain it to me."

[25]Then Joseph said to Pharaoh, "The dreams of Pharaoh are one and the same. God has revealed to Pharaoh what he is about to do. [26]The seven good cows are seven years, and the seven good heads of grain are seven years; it is one and the same dream. [27]The seven lean, ugly cows that came up afterward are seven years, and so are the seven worthless heads of grain scorched by the east wind: They are seven years of famine.

[28]"It is just as I said to Pharaoh: God has shown Pharaoh what he is about to do. [29]Seven years of great abundance are coming throughout the land of Egypt, [30]but seven years of famine will follow them. Then all the abundance in Egypt will be forgotten, and the famine will ravage the land. [31]The abundance in the land will not be remembered, because the famine that follows it will be so severe. [32]The reason the dream was given to Pharaoh in two forms is that the matter has been firmly decided by God, and God will do it soon."

MOST READ THE STORY of Joseph and Pharaoh's dreams and take away that God blessed Joseph because of his faithfulness and thereby made him one of the most powerful people in Egypt. I recognize this message, but I always looked at this story a little differently. My greedy human nature makes me think how lucky Pharaoh was that God told him there was going to be a drought and everything would die. I think it would be great if God did the same for us. I have had some strange dreams, but I've never been warned in my dreams that my crops would die.

If you think about it, there are many stories in the Bible in which God warned his people of destruction. God told Noah to build an ark, he rescued Lot from the destruction of Sodom and Gomorrah, and he sent Jonah to save Nineveh. It seems to us as Christians that God has forgotten about us in the twenty-first century. He never physically appears to us or gives us warnings. And if people today claim that they have seen the Lord, we dismiss them and group them with those who claim to have seen UFOs.

I will leave the claims of Jesus sightings to your discretion. But if you are like me and have never had a physical face-to-face chat with God, you may feel a little left out when you read the Bible. However, just because God is not appearing to us in dreams or physically riding shotgun in the tractor does not mean he is not guiding our lives. If you think about the time the Old Testament covers in history, God was not making daily appearances, at least according to recorded accounts. In biblical times he was working daily in his people's lives, and today he continues to do the same.

God does not call you on the phone and tell you how to live your life, but that doesn't mean he isn't always in control. Sometimes he influences our lives through other people. Have you ever had the experience where someone you really needed showed up at exactly the right time? Nonbelievers may call this coincidence, but as Christians we know that God controls the "coincidences" of our lives. While he might not be talking with you about last night's big game as you ride in the tractor, he is there with you everywhere you go, providing his love and guidance.

God did have one promise that was told numerous times to his believers in the Old Testament: he would send a savior. Today, we take comfort in the greatest prophecy of all time: that Jesus will return to take all believers to heaven. While God might not be coming to us in dreams anytime soon, we do have that promise of our future with him. And by living every day as a Christian, maybe we share a little of God's love through what we do.

Spiritual Milk

1 Peter 2:2–3

²Like newborn babies, crave pure spiritual milk, so that by it you may grow up in your salvation, ³now that you have tasted that the Lord is good.

WHEN I WAS GROWING UP, my dad was still a dairy farmer and we had many cows on our farm. When a new calf was born, it was put into a little pen separate from all the older calves and cows. Being the youngest on the farm, I was always given the job of teaching these new calves how to drink milk from a bottle, and eventually from a bucket. If you have ever taught a calf to drink, you may understand the trouble I had. Suffice it to say that I was not too sad to see my dad get out of dairy farming while I was still relatively young.

The calves were hungry, but often they did not want to drink the milk because they did not understand that they needed it to survive. I would try everything I could to get them to drink, but some calves were just stubborn. Eventually I would just open their mouths and dump down some milk. Then, once they learned that the milk was good for them, it was sometimes hard to pull the empty bottle away from the calves. They wanted more of this good, sweet milk. The calves soon learned that I would be there each day to feed them. Before long, they started to get excited every time I entered the barn.

God is like a farmer to us. He is there to take care of us, but sometimes we do not think that what he has to offer is good for us. Like those calves I fed that did not want the milk I provided, we think that we might be better off without God or that we can get by on our own. It may seem that we are doing fine, but then one day we realize that we need help from God, who has complete control of our lives. We drink his milk by learning more about him and making him part of our lives. At first, believing in God may seem different from the way we have lived our lives in the past, but when we start drinking the milk we see the difference and do not want to stop drinking.

Thankfully, God's bottle of milk is never empty. The more milk we drink, the better it will taste. When the calves on my father's farm grew big, they were put in with the older cows to fend for themselves and I lost track of them. But God is always there for us throughout our lives. He will never leave us. Unlike livestock, we have heaven to look forward to someday. When we die, God will bring us to heaven to live with him forever. Heaven will be perfect as we share it with God and everyone else who believed in him on earth. And fortunately, I will not have to feed any calves in heaven.

Saving the World

Genesis 7:1–10, 13–16 (NKJV)

[1]Then the Lord said to Noah, "Come into the ark, you and all your household, because I have seen that you are righteous before Me in this generation. [2]You shall take with you seven each of every clean animal, a male and his female; two each of animals that are unclean, a male and his female; [3]also seven each of birds of the air, male and female, to keep the species alive on the face of all the earth. [4]For after seven more days I will cause it to rain on the earth forty days and forty nights, and I will destroy from the face of the earth all living things that I have made." [5]And Noah did according to all that the Lord commanded him. [6]Noah was six hundred years old when the floodwaters were on the earth.

[7]So Noah, with his sons, his wife, and his sons' wives, went into the ark because of the waters of the flood. [8]Of clean animals, of animals that are unclean, of birds, and of everything that creeps on the earth, [9]two by two they went into the ark to Noah, male and female, as God had commanded Noah. [10]And it came to pass after seven days that the waters of the flood were on the earth.

[13]On the very same day Noah and Noah's sons, Shem, Ham, and Japheth, and Noah's wife and the three wives of his sons with them, entered the ark—[14]they and every beast after its kind, all cattle after their kind, every creeping thing that creeps on the earth after its kind, and every bird after its kind, every bird of every sort. [15]And they went into the ark to Noah, two by two, of all flesh in which is the breath of life. [16]So those that entered, male and female of all flesh, went in as God had commanded him; and the Lord shut him in.

DO YOU EVER GET SICK of feeding animals or hauling manure? When I think of Noah entering the ark, I think of Mike Rowe in the Discovery Channel show *Dirty Jobs*. The ark would have been a great place for Mike to visit. Imagine cramming every type of animal into a cruise ship. Now imagine how long it took Noah and his sons to ready that ship. They needed to prepare pens and raise and collect enough food for every animal and every person on the boat.

Sure, the flood must have been bad, but at least it only lasted forty days, right? However, when we look closer at Genesis we see that forty days was only the length of the rainstorm. Noah, his family, and all the animals actually spent a little over a year on the ark. That means they started with enough food for a year, and ended with enough manure for a year. I bet Noah was glad to set foot on dry land!

Noah was a man of faith. If God told you a flood was going to cover the entire earth and you needed to save it, would you? If God told you to start stocking a food supply to feed every animal for a year, would you do it? If God told you to build the biggest boat ever created, in the middle of dry land, would you do it? How many times has God told us to do something and we ignored him?

Thankfully, God probably will not ask us to do any favors that will save humanity. But he does give us some big jobs. We are told to love him, and love those around us. We need to serve others and do good in everything we do. Noah was not a great missionary. He did not convert all the evil people of the world. God gave him the mission to take care of his creation, and carry his ministry to those around him: his family.

What is God's ministry for you? Are you supposed to be like Moses and bring a nation back to God, or is your mission to care for God's creation around you? If your mission is the latter, there is still plenty of work to be done. Whether you are keeping your family's Christian faith strong or simply tending God's crops and animals, you are working for the Lord. We need to remember that even though we might not be saving the world from destruction, our small influence locally is very important to God.

Are You Wheat or Weeds?

Matthew 13:24–30, 36–43

²⁴Jesus told them another parable: "The kingdom of heaven is like a man who sowed good seed in his field. ²⁵But while everyone was sleeping, his enemy came and sowed weeds among the wheat, and went away. ²⁶When the wheat sprouted and formed heads, then the weeds also appeared.

²⁷"The owner's servants came to him and said, 'Sir, didn't you sow good seed in your field? Where then did the weeds come from?'

²⁸" 'An enemy did this,' he replied.

"The servants asked him, 'Do you want us to go and pull them up?'

²⁹" 'No,' he answered, 'because while you are pulling the weeds, you may root up the wheat with them. ³⁰Let both grow together until the harvest. At that time I will tell the harvesters: First collect the weeds and tie them in bundles to be burned; then gather the wheat and bring it into my barn.' "

³⁶Then he left the crowd and went into the house. His disciples came to him and said, "Explain to us the parable of the weeds in the field."

³⁷He answered, "The one who sowed the good seed is the Son of Man. ³⁸The field is the world, and the good seed stands for the sons of the kingdom. The weeds are the sons of the evil one, ³⁹and the enemy who sows them is the devil. The harvest is the end of the age, and the harvesters are angels.

⁴⁰"As the weeds are pulled up and burned in the fire, so it will be at the end of the age. ⁴¹The Son of Man will send out his angels, and they will weed out of his kingdom everything that causes sin and all who do evil. ⁴²They will throw them into the fiery furnace, where there will be weeping and gnashing of teeth. ⁴³Then the righteous will shine like the sun in the kingdom of their Father. He who has ears, let him hear."

EVERY YEAR IT SEEMS my fields of watermelon and muskmelon are full of weeds. When the plants are small we do a lot of cultivating and hoeing to keep the weeds out. But by the end of June the vines begin to spread out across the ground, changing the rows of plants to one giant mass. With over a month until harvest begins, the weeds take advantage of the situation and grow again. We could continue to hoe and pull weeds by hand, but we would have to walk on the melon vines. This would probably hurt the plants more than the weeds will, so we just let them grow.

In the parable of the weeds, the farmer could have really used some Roundup to kill off the weeds. But this would have killed all the wheat too. He was in the same predicament I am with my melons. So the farmer let the weeds grow up. For some of the wheat, the weeds may have been a problem because it was not strong enough to fight the weeds for nutrients. But other wheat probably grew stronger and better because it fought the weeds to win.

God works in a similar way in our lives. Surely God has the power to remove all of those who do not believe in him. But this would eliminate free choice and we would grow complacent without the struggles. There is no denying that sin takes people away from God. These people are just like the wheat that will grow less strongly because of the weeds choking it out. Many people in this world have heard the good news of Jesus, but they choose not to accept it. They find more important things to do, or think they can make it on their own.

I have always believed that anything that is not producing what is needed is a weed. Every person is born as wheat. We have the opportunity to come to God and believe. Some people's wheat might be stronger than ours, but that is okay. Our faith in God is all we need to produce. As our wheat continues to grow, we will slowly come closer to God.

Harvest day is coming, and the weeds will be separated from the wheat. God wants you to be part of his harvest. Are you putting your faith in him?

Controlling Your Bit

James 3:3–9

³When we put bits into the mouths of horses to make them obey us, we can turn the whole animal. ⁴Or take ships as an example. Although they are so large and are driven by strong winds, they are steered by a very small rudder wherever the pilot wants to go. ⁵Likewise the tongue is a small part of the body, but it makes great boasts. Consider what a great forest is set on fire by a small spark. ⁶The tongue also is a fire, a world of evil among the parts of the body. It corrupts the whole person, sets the whole course of his life on fire, and is itself set on fire by hell.

⁷All kinds of animals, birds, reptiles and creatures of the sea are being tamed and have been tamed by man, ⁸but no man can tame the tongue. It is a restless evil, full of deadly poison.

⁹With the tongue we praise our Lord and Father, and with it we curse men, who have been made in God's likeness.

MANY FARMERS TODAY cannot relate to training horses except in certain ranching regions or other specialty uses. Horses used to be the lifeblood of all farmers, but today they have lost their vital significance for most farms. Yet our grandparents were probably very familiar with horses. Without them, they simply could not have farmed.

Horses were a vital part of farms before the truck or tractor. Horses plowed the field, pulled the wagons during harvest, and carried the harvest to town in a wagon. They took the family to church on Sunday and provided transportation around the farm. The bit, such a small tool, was vital for the training and control of the animal. Despite its small size, it controlled one of the most powerful "machines" on the farm. Today, few farms use horses to plow the fields, but we still hold lots of power in our hands. A two-hundred-horsepower tractor needs a qualified driver who can properly control it or else it will not do its intended task.

The passage above talks about training our tongue or mouth. God wants us to use it to praise him, but how often do we use it for evil purposes? Sure, we go to church on Sunday and sing a few hymns, but what about the rest of the week? There are plenty of ways we misuse our mouth. We may spread rumors, tell lies, talk poorly about others, or promote other evils. It is easy to forget about our duty as Christians to live God-pleasing lives, but we need to continually think about how we are using our mouth.

Instead using our mouths to speak poorly of others, we have the opportunity to share good words. When others are spreading rumors, do you join in or do you stand up for the person being ridiculed? Do you share the word of God with those around you who need it? Do you offer yourself as a friend and encourager for those who need you?

We have the opportunity to use our mouth to God's glory. It may be a small body part, but it holds the power to spread either good or evil. Be sure to make the right choice.

Know Your Master

Isaiah 1: 2–3, 11–18

[2] Hear, O heavens! Listen, O earth!
For the LORD has spoken:
"I reared children and brought them up,
but they have rebelled against me.
[3] The ox knows his master,
the donkey his owner's manger,
but Israel does not know,
my people do not understand."

[11] "The multitude of your sacrifices—
what are they to me?" says the LORD.
"I have more than enough of burnt offerings,
of rams and the fat of fattened animals;
I have no pleasure
in the blood of bulls and lambs and goats.
[12] When you come to appear before me,
who has asked this of you,
this trampling of my courts?
[13] Stop bringing meaningless offerings!
Your incense is detestable to me.
New Moons, Sabbaths and convocations—
I cannot bear your evil assemblies.
[14] Your New Moon festivals and your appointed feasts
my soul hates.
They have become a burden to me;
I am weary of bearing them.
[15] When you spread out your hands in prayer,
I will hide my eyes from you;
even if you offer many prayers,

I will not listen.

Your hands are full of blood;

¹⁶ wash and make yourselves clean.

Take your evil deeds

out of my sight!

Stop doing wrong,

¹⁷ learn to do right!

Seek justice,

encourage the oppressed.

Defend the cause of the fatherless,

plead the case of the widow.

¹⁸ "Come now, let us reason together,"

says the LORD.

"Though your sins are like scarlet,

they shall be as white as snow;

though they are red as crimson,

they shall be like wool."

WE CAN ALL GET frustrated by how much trouble livestock can cause sometimes. Yet the animals still know that the farmer is there to care for them and that he or she is the master. They may try to kick you on the way, but they rely on you for food, shelter, and care. Human beings are similar. Why is it so hard for us to recognize that God is our master?

Judah was struggling with the same problem. While they did offer God sacrifices and prayer, there was no heart behind it. They were just going through the motions. God was frustrated with them. If livestock could figure out who their master was, why couldn't God's chosen people figure out that God deserved their wholehearted thankfulness? They offered God sacrifices, but they did not follow up and try to live righteous lives.

As Christians, we know that we cannot live a life good enough to earn salvation. No matter how many good things we do, we cannot make up for the many more evil things we do. That is why we need to recognize our master. Only through humbling ourselves and asking for forgiveness can we be given the gift of eternal life.

If we cannot earn our salvation, why should we even bother trying to be a servant and helping others? We should help others because it is pleasing to God. It is just the right thing to do. While works do not earn us salvation or give us bonus points, they do bring us closer to God. God does great things for his people, but he uses us to accomplish many of those things.

What is the true reason you serve God today? Do you go to church to praise and learn about God, or are you just going through the motions? Are you serving others to the glory of God, or do you simply serve because it looks good to others? Know your master, and live your life for him.

Got Meat?

Genesis 9:1–6

[1]Then God blessed Noah and his sons, saying to them, "Be fruitful and increase in number and fill the earth. [2]The fear and dread of you will fall upon all the beasts of the earth and all the birds of the air, upon every creature that moves along the ground, and upon all the fish of the sea; they are given into your hands. [3]Everything that lives and moves will be food for you. Just as I gave you the green plants, I now give you everything.

[4]"But you must not eat meat that has its lifeblood still in it. [5]And for your lifeblood I will surely demand an accounting. I will demand an accounting from every animal. And from each man, too, I will demand an accounting for the life of his fellow man.

> [6]"Whoever sheds the blood of man,
> by man shall his blood be shed;
> for in the image of God
> has God made man."

"YOU SHALL NOT MURDER." We are all familiar with this commandment. God tells us not to kill one another. But animals are another thing, right? Sometimes it can be confusing. Animal-rights groups have blasted farmers for decades for using animals for food and other uses. Some vegetarians say they decided never to eat meat again after seeing how farm animals are treated. Nutrition debates sometimes include statements that meat is not natural or healthy for humans.

As Christian farmers, we can sometimes wonder if maybe we are doing something wrong raising meat as food. Sure, most people today eat meat, but are we going against God's will? Is our daily work a sin against God?

When Noah left the ark, God gave the earth a new start. Interestingly, God gave Noah and his family a new set of rules regarding animals. Just as

God had given Adam all the green plants of the earth to eat in the Garden of Eden, now God was giving Noah the meat of the land also.

God gave his people the fruit of the land, both breathing and green. When he gave Adam the power to rule over the land in the Garden of Eden, he gave Adam the responsibility to care for his creation. As farmers today, we continue that work. As farmers, we must take care of the land and animals. Even though livestock is raised to eventually be killed, we are to treat livestock with respect until that time comes.

Our job is also to care for God's most prized creation: humanity. By raising food and other products for our fellow humans, we are caring for them. God gave us the authority to rule and to care. Continue in your work knowing that you are fulfilling the work of the Lord.

Talents

Matthew 25:14–30 (NKJV)

[14]"For the kingdom of heaven is like a man traveling to a far country, who called his own servants and delivered his goods to them. [15]And to one he gave five talents, to another two, and to another one, to each according to his own ability; and immediately he went on a journey. [16]Then he who had received the five talents went and traded with them, and made another five talents. [17]And likewise he who had received two gained two more also. [18]But he who had received one went and dug in the ground, and hid his lord's money. [19]After a long time the lord of those servants came and settled accounts with them.

[20]"So he who had received five talents came and brought five other talents, saying, 'Lord, you delivered to me five talents; look, I have gained five more talents besides them.' [21]His lord said to him, 'Well done, good and faithful servant; you were faithful over a few things, I will make you ruler over many things. Enter into the joy of your lord.' [22]He also who had received two talents came and said, 'Lord, you delivered to me two talents; look, I have gained two more talents besides them.' [23]His lord said to him, 'Well done, good and faithful servant; you have been faithful over a few things, I will make you ruler over many things. Enter into the joy of your lord.'

[24]"Then he who had received the one talent came and said, 'Lord, I knew you to be a hard man, reaping where you have not sown, and gathering where you have not scattered seed. [25]And I was afraid, and went and hid your talent in the ground. Look, there you have what is yours.'

[26]"But his lord answered and said to him, 'You wicked and lazy servant, you knew that I reap where I have not sown, and gather where I have not scattered seed. [27]So you ought to have deposited my money with the bankers, and at my coming I would have received back my own with interest. [28]Therefore take the talent from him, and give it to him who has ten talents.

[29]" 'For to everyone who has, more will be given, and he will have abundance; but from him who does not have, even what he has will be taken away. [30]And cast the unprofitable servant into the outer darkness. There will be weeping and gnashing of teeth.' "

WE KNOW THAT we can serve God in whatever occupation we choose. But as farmers, sometimes it can feel like we are not very close to God in our work, and we may wonder how we are really serving God. Sure, we are feeding the world, but how is each of us really making a difference in the world? If we stopped farming today there would not be a noticeable change in the world's supply of food, and in reality almost no one besides a few friends and neighbors would even notice our absence.

The parable of the talents demonstrates that God gives each of us different gifts. For some it is singing, for others it is writing, and for some it is being able to farm (and have the emotional strength to survive the tough times). We do not have to be preachers to share God's love; we simply need to use what he has given us to the best of our ability.

In our role as farmers, God expects a lot from us. Does that mean we need to have the most productive land so that we can produce the most food off the smallest area? Not necessarily. If your poor farming practices are destroying the land or you are mistreating your livestock, you are not using your abilities to God's glory. But when we care for our God-given gifts and use them for the good of both ourselves and others, then we are serving God.

We are tasked with not only watching God's resources, but also helping to grow them. The servant who only received one talent went away and did not use it for fear that he might hurt or lose it. But when the master heard what he had done, he was furious. He was so angry that he called the servant lazy and wicked, and threw him into the darkness. That may seem harsh for a servant who had good intentions, but God tells us that we have a mission, and this parable makes it clear that he expects us to fulfill it.

While our occupation is farming, God intends that we do much more with our lives. Because we are Christians, God expects us to serve him. We do not need to be ministers to lead a Bible study or teach Sunday school. We can share the good news of Jesus with friends, and keep our families in a Christian home. Furthermore, we can live a life of servanthood. When your neighbor needs a hand fixing a tractor or rounding up some escaped livestock, will you be willing to help? God has blessed us in many ways, and we must use them to improve his kingdom.

In your roles as a farmer and as a Christian, make sure you use your talents to the glory of God.

Not the Hired Hand

John 10:11–18

[11]"I am the good shepherd. The good shepherd lays down his life for the sheep. [12]The hired hand is not the shepherd and does not own the sheep. So when he sees the wolf coming, he abandons the sheep and runs away. Then the wolf attacks the flock and scatters it. [13]The man runs away because he is a hired hand and cares nothing for the sheep.

[14]"I am the good shepherd; I know my sheep and my sheep know me— [15]just as the Father knows me and I know the Father—and I lay down my life for the sheep. [16]I have other sheep that are not of this sheep pen. I must bring them also. They too will listen to my voice, and there shall be one flock and one shepherd. [17]The reason my Father loves me is that I lay down my life— only to take it up again. [18]No one takes it from me, but I lay it down of my own accord. I have authority to lay it down and authority to take it up again. This command I received from my Father."

HAVE YOU EVER HAD to hire people to work at your farm? Maybe you just hired someone for a few days to help bale hay, or maybe you needed to hire someone to do the third shift milking every day. Some employees do a great job, but others can be a source of frustration when you have to rely on someone else to do your work.

In my experience, it seems like employees rarely do the same quality of job as I would do. This is not because I believe I am great at what I do and that no one can match me. It's because, being the owner of my business, I know exactly how I want to run it. While employees can do their best to match my expectations, they cannot always do everything exactly how I would do it. I have had many great employees who took pride in their work and felt a sense of ownership. However, whether they did an excellent job or just an average job, in the end they knew they would still get a paycheck.

Fortunately, when God knew that his people needed someone to save them from their sin, he did not send the hired man. He sent Jesus, his one and only son. He sent many hired men and women before and after Jesus, such as the prophets and apostles. These hired workers were certainly important to God's ministry. But, like the hired shepherd who ran away when the wolf came, many of these leaders let their fear and sin get in the way, and they made mistakes. Moses struck a rock for water without trusting God, Jonah ran away from God's ministry, and Peter denied even knowing Jesus. While the many popular heroes of the Bible and even today were great leaders, they were human and had human flaws.

As sinful humans, we needed the master to come and save us. We needed someone who would do the job right and not run away from fear or danger. Jesus certainly knew that if he did not do his job, he would lose all people. Thankfully, Jesus was the ultimate owner and took the responsibility for all our sins. His perfect life, ending with death on the cross, was something that no hired man could have done. Because of his death and resurrection, we have the gift of victory over death and the promise of salvation if we believe in Jesus.

Talking Donkeys

Numbers 22:22–33

[22]But God was very angry when he went, and the angel of the LORD stood in the road to oppose him. Balaam was riding on his donkey, and his two servants were with him. [23]When the donkey saw the angel of the LORD standing in the road with a drawn sword in his hand, she turned off the road into a field. Balaam beat her to get her back on the road.

[24]Then the angel of the LORD stood in a narrow path between two vineyards, with walls on both sides. [25]When the donkey saw the angel of the LORD, she pressed close to the wall, crushing Balaam's foot against it. So he beat her again.

[26]Then the angel of the LORD moved on ahead and stood in a narrow place where there was no room to turn, either to the right or to the left. [27]When the donkey saw the angel of the LORD, she lay down under Balaam, and he was angry and beat her with his staff. [28]Then the LORD opened the donkey's mouth, and she said to Balaam, "What have I done to you to make you beat me these three times?"

[29]Balaam answered the donkey, "You have made a fool of me! If I had a sword in my hand, I would kill you right now."

[30]The donkey said to Balaam, "Am I not your own donkey, which you have always ridden, to this day? Have I been in the habit of doing this to you?"

"No," he said.

[31]Then the LORD opened Balaam's eyes, and he saw the angel of the LORD standing in the road with his sword drawn. So he bowed low and fell facedown.

[32]The angel of the LORD asked him, "Why have you beaten your donkey these three times? I have come here to oppose you because your path is a reckless one before me. [33]The donkey saw me and turned away from me these three times. If she had not turned away, I would certainly have killed you by now, but I would have spared her."

BALAAM WAS NOT having a good day. While the Bible does not specifically say why, God was mad at Balaam because his path was a reckless one. Suddenly, on a journey to visit a bad king, his donkey started acting strange because an angel was blocking the path. His donkey saw the angel, but Balaam could not. Balaam responded by beating his donkey until it returned to the path.

This happened two more times, and Balaam was getting angry. After the third time, the donkey (and God) had had enough. Suddenly, the donkey spoke to Balaam and asked him why he kept beating her. Balaam, seemingly unimpressed by the fact that his donkey was talking to him, got in an argument with his donkey. But suddenly God opened Balaam's eyes and he saw that the donkey had actually been protecting him.

Very few farmers have had a two-way conversation with their animals. This Old Testament story may seem like a strange way for God to intervene in someone's life. But God does intervene in our lives, even if it is not through talking animals. Like Balaam, we often do not see the problem that is right in front of us. Sometimes we are so consumed with our own lives that we miss it, and sometimes we simply do not know what events may be coming. God does know what we face, and he puts people, events, and resources in our lives to help guide us.

Sometimes we may be lacking in our faith, and God will bring us back closer to him through people around us or through important events. Or he may put delays in our lives to make things work for the best. Maybe the last time your car broke down God did this to help you avoid getting in a nasty accident a mile down the road. God does everything for a reason, whether it is great or small.

When something bad does happen, we need to take time to look for the good. When a part breaks and I have to wait a few minutes before it is delivered, I will take that time to read a devotion. This is a great way for me to use the time: I am forced to slow down and make sure God is still in my life. Doing this also helps me feel comforted that everything will work out. God is in control and I need to trust him.

What do you do when God intervenes in your life?

Measuring a Sacrifice

Genesis 4:2b–7

²ᵇNow Abel kept flocks, and Cain worked the soil. ³In the course of time Cain brought some of the fruits of the soil as an offering to the LORD. ⁴And Abel also brought an offering—fat portions from some of the firstborn of his flock. The LORD looked with favor on Abel and his offering, ⁵but on Cain and his offering he did not look with favor. So Cain was very angry, and his face was downcast.

⁶Then the LORD said to Cain, "Why are you angry? Why is your face downcast? ⁷If you do what is right, will you not be accepted? But if you do not do what is right, sin is crouching at your door; it desires to have you, but you must rule over it."

IT IS INTERESTING to see how important farming was so early in the Bible. Adam and Eve's first two sons were farmers. Abel was a herdsman and Cain was a crop farmer. They each had a specialty and served the Lord in what they did. Soon it came time for them to bring their first fruits to God.

The Bible does not state clearly that Cain's offering was bad. While it comments that Abel's was "fat portions from some of the firstborn of his flock," Cain's is simply described as "some of the fruits of the soil." But God did not look equally on both gifts.

Was it that God preferred meat to a vegetarian entrée? Should Cain have found a different occupation so that he could give more to God? Of course not. God told him that he was not doing what was right. While many believe that Cain's problem of giving was that he only gave God the leftovers, the problem probably lay with what was in Cain's heart.

Cain became angry when God did not accept his gift. Cain's problem was that he was only giving to get glory. When Abel got the glory instead, Cain eventually murdered him because of his jealousy. God wanted Cain to give from his heart. Certainly his gifts of fruits were not bad; the problem lay in his motivation.

Millenniums later we still struggle with the same problem. What motivates us to put money in the offering plate each week? Why do we donate to charity? Why do we volunteer our time to those in need? Is it so that we will not feel cheap in passing the plate without giving? Is it so that we can look good by having our name printed in the annual newsletter as a platinum donor? Is it so that we will get recognized as an outstanding volunteer or look good to our friends?

All of these actions and gifts are certainly important, but we need to do them for the right reason. We need to give time and money for the glory of God. We should not be looking for a pat on the back or a thank you. God knows what we have done to serve him. If we donate a million dollars, but for the wrong reason, will God be pleased with our gift? While there is certainly nothing wrong with recognition, we need to do God's work for *his* glory.

Hopefully you do your work as a farmer to serve God. You do your work not because you want to be the best farmer, one that everyone envies, but because you are caring for God's land and creatures. Part of this task is to provide for your family and those around you. Sometimes God will bless your work with an abundant harvest, and there will be years when God will check your humility. But, whether the task is great or small, if you work to please God, then you have put your focus in the right place.

Life Is Not Perfect If You Need an Ark

Genesis 7:17–8:4

[17]For forty days the flood kept coming on the earth, and as the waters increased they lifted the ark high above the earth. [18]The waters rose and increased greatly on the earth, and the ark floated on the surface of the water. [19]They rose greatly on the earth, and all the high mountains under the entire heavens were covered. [20]The waters rose and covered the mountains to a depth of more than fifteen cubits. [21]Every living thing that moved on land perished—birds, livestock, wild animals, all the creatures that swarm over the earth, and all mankind. [22]Everything on dry land that had the breath of life in its nostrils died. [23]Every living thing on the face of the earth was wiped out; people and animals and the creatures that move along the ground and the birds were wiped from the earth. Only Noah was left, and those with him in the ark.

[24]The waters flooded the earth for a hundred and fifty days.

[8:1]But God remembered Noah and all the wild animals and the livestock that were with him in the ark, and he sent a wind over the earth, and the waters receded. [2]Now the springs of the deep and the floodgates of the heavens had been closed, and the rain had stopped falling from the sky. [3]The water receded steadily from the earth. At the end of the hundred and fifty days the water had gone down, [4]and on the seventeenth day of the seventh month the ark came to rest on the mountains of Ararat.

THE SPRING OF 2011 was especially tough for farmers around the country. By May 1, only about fifteen percent of the total U.S. corn acreage was planted. Farmers struggled with abnormally cold temperatures throughout April, and with the amount of April showers we should have seen lots of May flowers.

In Wisconsin, we were pretty down about the weather and being set back a few weeks with planting. Yet our situation was ideal compared to what farmers in many other states were dealing with. Large parts of Alabama and surrounding states were coping with one of the largest outbreaks of tornados in history, which killed hundreds of people and destroyed entire towns in a single afternoon. In other areas, flooding was destroying fields, homes, and property. News reports showed floods spreading as far as seven miles from waterways, into places that had never flooded before.

Back in Wisconsin, we had a reality check. Being unable to plant suddenly seemed much less severe than it had before. Think about Noah. He was probably having a good life before the flood. His farm was prosperous, his sons had all married and were farming with him on the family farm, and (being six hundred years old) the farm had already reached Century Farm status a few times over. Yet God told Noah that almost everything he had worked so hard to build would be destroyed. His house, his fences, the vineyards he had so carefully tilled, and even the toolshed Ham and Shem had built as a Father's Day gift would be destroyed.

Bad though Noah's situation was, God had a plan. Through Noah, God would repopulate the world. Noah would become the father of all future humanity. Eventually, God would restore Noah's farm in a different region, where he would rebuild his life. While we know the end of the story, and know that everything will work out, Noah was probably pretty frustrated thinking his life was going to be destroyed. But rather than trying to bargain with God, he spent his time and energy trusting God by building the ark.

As farmers, we know there are going to be tough seasons. There will be years when we will lose money. There will be disasters that will destroy our property. There will even be times when God takes loved ones away from us. But as Christians we know that God has a plan. We might not understand it now, but we know that if we trust in God he will use it to his glory. While we may not always be blessed with an earthly reward, we know that if we stay strong in faith we will eventually be given the ultimate gift of heaven. So what will you do the next time your farming day is not quite perfect?

An Empty Feeling

Acts 1:9–11

[9]After he said this, he was taken up before their very eyes, and a cloud hid him from their sight.

[10]They were looking intently up into the sky as he was going, when suddenly two men dressed in white stood beside them. [11]"Men of Galilee," they said, "why do you stand here looking into the sky? This same Jesus, who has been taken from you into heaven, will come back in the same way you have seen him go into heaven."

OCTOBER 31 IS ALWAYS an exciting day at our farm. It is the final day of our farm market's produce season. After five intense months of hard work, everything suddenly comes to a close. While we enjoy our jobs, there is a sense of relief that another season has passed. We know there is still work ahead to close everything up, but the easing of pressure is thrilling.

Then November 1 arrives. Months of preparation, setup, and harvesting are mostly removed in a single morning. Our farm suddenly looks bare. At noon our picking crew leaves for the last time, not to return until the following June, and I feel a sort of emptiness. Though I am ready for a break, it is an adjustment to suddenly feel all alone. I almost wish that it was not over yet . . . almost!

After Jesus ascended into heaven, the disciples had some of the same feelings I do each year at the end of produce season. They had spent three years following Jesus, and had witnessed many great things. Jesus had spent time teaching them, and they had showed signs of growth. Then he was suddenly taken from them and hung on a cross. While I might feel a little empty at the end of a successful season, they must have felt really confused when their leader was tortured and crucified as a criminal.

The disciples reacted with a feeling of loss and confusion, and they went and locked themselves in a room. They did not know what to do next. As Jesus appeared to them over the next forty days, he continued to prepare them for their ministry without him. He gave them some time to regroup, and then he commissioned them to go and tell his story to the world.

In Acts 1, Jesus ascended into heaven. The disciples, just like me, were experiencing loss again. But suddenly two angels brought them back to reality: "Men of Galilee," they said, "why do you stand here looking into the sky? This same Jesus, who has been taken from you into heaven, will come back in the same way you have seen him go into heaven."

The disciples were far from being done with their work. In fact, their work was about to get much more important. Before, they had been Jesus' followers and helpers. But without his physical presence, they were now the ones in charge. They were the face of the organization. Jesus' mission was now *their* mission. The angels told the disciples there was no time to waste. Jesus would be back, but they needed to start preparing the world for that time.

When does your day of sky-gazing happen? If you are a cold-climate farmer, winter might be a slower time for you. Weekends, nights, or other times might leave open time for you to fill. While it is easy to fill so many of our days with work, God also gives us time to serve him. Our work for God is never over, no matter how old we get, so use the time you have to serve him. Whether in work or play, we are God's servants every day.

Neighborhood Rumors

Matthew 8:5–13

[5]When Jesus had entered Capernaum, a centurion came to him, asking for help. [6]"Lord," he said, "my servant lies at home paralyzed, suffering terribly."

[7]Jesus said to him, "Shall I come and heal him?"

[8]The centurion replied, "Lord, I do not deserve to have you come under my roof. But just say the word, and my servant will be healed. [9]For I myself am a man under authority, with soldiers under me. I tell this one, 'Go,' and he goes; and that one, 'Come,' and he comes. I say to my servant, 'Do this,' and he does it."

[10]When Jesus heard this, he was amazed and said to those following him, "Truly I tell you, I have not found anyone in Israel with such great faith. [11]I say to you that many will come from the east and the west, and will take their places at the feast with Abraham, Isaac and Jacob in the kingdom of heaven. [12]But the subjects of the kingdom will be thrown outside, into the darkness, where there will be weeping and gnashing of teeth."

[13]Then Jesus said to the centurion, "Go! Let it be done just as you believed it would." And his servant was healed at that moment.

HAVE YOU HEARD about that guy a few counties away who is getting three hundred bushels of corn to the acre this year? What about the reports that the price of milk will go over $25 per hundredweight by Christmas? Did you see that the new John Deere grain buggy can haul two full semi loads at a time? How about that new GPS system that allows you to operate without employees—the tractors just drive themselves?

It is pretty easy to be skeptical sometimes, and that is probably a good thing. Especially in a rural neighborhood, false rumors can travel fast. As the story gets told and retold, it only gets better. Those doing the telling may not purposely beef up a story, but no one wants to tell a boring story!

In Matthew 8 we hear a story about a centurion who had heard about Jesus. While Matthew does not directly tell us, I am willing to guess that the centurion had heard many stories about Jesus. Maybe he had heard things such as how Jesus had healed a man with leprosy, and made the blind see and the deaf hear. Or maybe the stories had told of Jesus feeding thousands of people with a few loaves of bread and a couple of fish, turning jars of water into wine, or commanding a storm to be quiet.

I don't know about you, but I think I would believe three-hundred-bushel corn stories long before I would believe the stories told about this guy Jesus. Yet the centurion still believed even without seeing. He believed the stories about Jesus were more than just rumors. He was a man in authority, but his faith in the powers of Jesus was strong. He believed so strongly that he knew Jesus did not need to come to his home. A word was all it would take.

The power of Jesus is so much more than just a rumor. We can be assured that what he has done is the living truth. At times we may have doubts about the truth of the Bible. It can be easy to question whether the Bible is reality or just a bunch of improved stories. Thankfully, God provides proofs. Whether they are the hundreds of prophecies that Jesus fulfilled or the way God continues to work in our lives, we know that Jesus is the truth.

We know the truth, and we have our fellow Christians to support us in it. But do we take time to spread the story of the Bible and Jesus' saving grace? Or is the Bible a story we forget to spread around? A savior who died so we might have eternal life: that sounds like a story that does not need any improving.

Connected to the Stem

John 15:1–11

[1]"I am the true vine, and my Father is the gardener. [2]He cuts off every branch in me that bears no fruit, while every branch that does bear fruit he prunes so that it will be even more fruitful. [3]You are already clean because of the word I have spoken to you. [4]Remain in me, as I also remain in you. No branch can bear fruit by itself; it must remain in the vine. Neither can you bear fruit unless you remain in me.

[5]"I am the vine; you are the branches. If you remain in me and I in you, you will bear much fruit; apart from me you can do nothing. [6]If you do not remain in me, you are like a branch that is thrown away and withers; such branches are picked up, thrown into the fire and burned. [7]If you remain in me and my words remain in you, ask whatever you wish, and it will be done for you. [8]This is to my Father's glory, that you bear much fruit, showing yourselves to be my disciples.

[9]"As the Father has loved me, so have I loved you. Now remain in my love. [10]If you keep my commands, you will remain in my love, just as I have kept my Father's commands and remain in his love. [11]I have told you this so that my joy may be in you and that your joy may be complete."

AS A VEGETABLE FARMER for many years, I am always amazed at the short shelf life of perishable crops. Take a look at green beans, for example. Once a green bean reaches maturity, it can usually sit on the plant for a week or more before it becomes overripe. Connected to the plant, it continues to receive water and nutrients, and sustains great quality. It will continue to grow a little each day, but this is a relatively slow ripening process compared to some other produce such as sweet corn, which ripens quickly.

However, once you pick a green bean everything changes. Once the bean is cut from the plant, the life source ends and that bean begins breaking down. If it's not put directly into cold storage, in just a day or two the bean will be soft, wrinkled, and unappetizing. Had that bean still been on the plant, it would have been fine for that period of time. Picking the bean was its death sentence.

Being a follower of Jesus is like being a green bean. If we follow him and remain in him, we are connected to him. We can continue to grow in our faith, enjoy the benefits of a relationship with Christ, and walk hand in hand with God. But sometimes we decide that we do not need that connection. We decide not to follow God's commands, we ignore our Christian faith, and we separate ourselves from Jesus. We think we know what we are doing or that we can survive on our own.

When we separate from Jesus, we suffer, just as the bean does when it is picked from the plant. We may be able to fool ourselves for a short time that we can survive. However, it does not take us long to realize that we cannot live without our life source. We wither and die. Without believing in Jesus as our savior, we are sent to the eternal fire of hell. That might be a scary thought, but it is a thought we cannot deny.

"If you remain in me and I in you, you will bear much fruit." I pray that you may choose to stay connected to Christ. Not only will you thrive spiritually; you will also have the opportunity to produce more fruit by sharing Christ with others. Sharing Christ can take many forms. You may just share love by helping others on a daily basis, or you may use more organized methods of teaching others about God. You may introduce a friend to Jesus, or you may travel around the world to bring Christ to a difficult culture. Whatever fruit you bear, may it be for Christ. All the fruit we bear comes from the power of the vine as we do his work.

Passing Through God's Land

Psalm 24:1–2

¹The earth is the LORD's, and everything in it,
the world, and all who live in it;
²for he founded it on the seas
and established it on the waters.

IN MY FIRST COLLEGE agribusiness class I learned about the cycle of a typical family farm. The cycle was described like this: each year a farm makes profit, money is taken and reinvested into the farm, which allows the farm to grow. Assuming all else remains equal, the farm continues to be able to add more income and grow. Any income beyond what is needed to cover family expenses is reinvested into more land, machinery, and equipment, which then make the farm more profitable.

Through this entire process, wealth is continually accumulated but is never really realized by the owner because all money was reinvested into the farm. And when the farmer finally retires and dies, what has all this wealth gained him? As the saying goes, "you can't take it with you."

As farmers we spend many years of our lives toiling, which certainly is not a bad thing. Part of our purpose is to provide and work for the betterment of all. However, what is our motivation for what we do? Are we working only to gain status? Does our farm expand because we need to expand or because we simply want more? Growth and success are not necessarily bad, but it is important to remember that our time here is limited. Our gifts and bounty should be used to glorify God.

My grandpa used to say, "We don't own the land; God just lets us work it as we are passing through." How true that is! Your farm fields have existed as soil since God created the heavens and the earth. Long after you are gone, they will continue to be there. If you think land is yours, you are mistaken. God is simply allowing you to take care of it.

Taking care of God's land comes with great responsibility. Essentially, we are doing his work. Every time we till the soil, we are tilling for God. Every time we plant the soil, we are planting for God. Every time we harvest the crop, we are harvesting for God. When we carefully manage the soil or do things to harm it, we are choosing how we care for God's land.

God's creation does not stop with the land. When we care for livestock, we are also caring for his creatures. "The earth is the LORD's, and everything in it." By properly feeding and providing good health care for our animals, we care for his creation.

God has put great trust in us to care for his creation: we need to take that job seriously. God expects us to care for his creation with diligence, but we should not let greed overtake us. We should always remember to share our gifts with him. As our farms produce bounty, let our bounty work for the Lord. From God it came, and to God it will return.

When Disaster Strikes

Job 1:13–22

[13]One day when Job's sons and daughters were feasting and drinking wine at the oldest brother's house, [14]a messenger came to Job and said, "The oxen were plowing and the donkeys were grazing nearby, [15]and the Sabeans attacked and carried them off. They put the servants to the sword, and I am the only one who has escaped to tell you!"

[16]While he was still speaking, another messenger came and said, "The fire of God fell from the sky and burned up the sheep and the servants, and I am the only one who has escaped to tell you!"

[17]While he was still speaking, another messenger came and said, "The Chaldeans formed three raiding parties and swept down on your camels and carried them off. They put the servants to the sword, and I am the only one who has escaped to tell you!"

[18]While he was still speaking, yet another messenger came and said, "Your sons and daughters were feasting and drinking wine at the oldest brother's house, [19]when suddenly a mighty wind swept in from the desert and struck the four corners of the house. It collapsed on them and they are dead, and I am the only one who has escaped to tell you!"

[20]At this, Job got up and tore his robe and shaved his head. Then he fell to the ground in worship [21]and said:

> "Naked I came from my mother's womb,
> and naked I will depart.
> The LORD gave and the LORD has taken away;
> may the name of the LORD be praised."

[22]In all this, Job did not sin by charging God with wrongdoing.

HAVE YOU EVER HAD one of those years? Maybe it rained all spring and all the crops were planted late. Half the farm almost washed away with the flooding. Then, when the rain did stop, it did not rain for two months, and oppressive heat not only dried everything but also made it miserable to work. Frost came early and killed the few crops that had grown before they reached full maturity. When you finally scraped in a meager harvest, the market prices dropped and you were paid next to nothing. This type of scenario probably sounds familiar to most farmers at some point in time, and maybe more familiar than we would like.

The good news is that we are not the first farmers to deal with such troubles. The Old Testament book of Job describes a very low point in Job's life. He was a successful farmer, with lots of land and livestock. He was considered a great success by those around him. Despite his success, Job was not conceited. Read chapter one of Job for the full story, but in short he always kept his faith and glory pointed to God. He praised God daily, and repented even when he thought he had done no wrong. Do you give God that kind of attention?

One day God allowed the devil to test Job. The devil sent raiders and disasters to kill his flocks, donkeys, camels, servants, and children. Everything Job had was gone . . . everything except his faith. What was Job's response to this disaster? He praised God. He realized that everything he had had was a gift from God, and if God decided to take it back then so be it.

The last time your crops flooded, hail killed a growing crop, or a sickness moved through your herd, did you praise God? If you are like me, praise was probably the *last* thing on your mind! It is much easier to blame God for such misfortune. But if we stop and look around us, we may still realize we are surrounded by blessings. We have our barns, homes, our own lives, and many other possessions to rebuild and continue. We have friends, family, and our church to help us through the struggle.

Even if all these blessing are removed, we have one blessing that will never be taken away: Jesus. See, Jesus was a guy who went through some bad times too. Despite being perfect, he was crucified on a cross. But because of that injustice, we have the assurance of heaven if we believe in him as our savior. While it can be hard at the time of disaster, we need to remember that heaven is far greater than a few extra dollars, a nicer house, or more possessions here on earth. Heaven is eternal greatness, and the alternative is horrendous.

I guarantee that you will have more tough days in the future. But God will send sunny days here on earth, and when our life ends here we will have the ultimate blessing for eternity. Now *that* is worth waiting for!

Using Your Specialty

1 Corinthians 12:4–11

⁴There are different kinds of gifts, but the same Spirit distributes them. ⁵There are different kinds of service, but the same Lord. ⁶There are different kinds of working, but in all of them and in everyone it is the same God at work.

⁷Now to each one the manifestation of the Spirit is given for the common good. ⁸To one there is given through the Spirit a message of wisdom, to another a message of knowledge by means of the same Spirit, ⁹to another faith by the same Spirit, to another gifts of healing by that one Spirit, ¹⁰to another miraculous powers, to another prophecy, to another distinguishing between spirits, to another speaking in different kinds of tongues, and to still another the interpretation of tongues. ¹¹All these are the work of one and the same Spirit, and he distributes them to each one, just as he determines.

MANY FAMILY FARMS today are owned and run by multiple family members. Parents, children, and siblings work side by side. As a family they work to complete the tasks of the farm. However, the way families go about this job can vary significantly.

Sometimes all farm tasks are managed by the oldest generation. The mother or father hands out tasks and asks for little input as the work is completed. In other cases, everyone shares in the work, but no one knows who is responsible for what task and everyone tries to do the same work. This can work for a while, but sometimes people become frustrated as work is done twice, people are stepping over each other, or tasks get completely missed. On other farms, everyone has a specialty. One person may be in charge of the livestock, another the crops, and another manages the finances. Everyone may help each other when needed, but each person uses his or her skills to better the farm.

When Paul wrote to the Corinthians, he described something very similar for the church. Just as everyone on a family farm may not be good at managing the books, everyone in a church might not be the best at giving a sermon on Sunday morning. God blesses each of us with different gifts.

Look around your church. As your gaze falls on each person, think about where their skills lie. How do they contribute to the success of your church? Some may be good at cooking dinners, others at teaching Sunday school, and still others might like keeping the grass mowed. Some may lead a Bible study, some may like committee meetings, and some may enjoy reaching out to the community. When you look at the wide range of skills, it can be amazing what God has brought together in your church.

Now that you have looked at those around you, ask yourself what your mission is. Why has God placed you in your church? What does he want you to accomplish? Why did he not lead you to join a different church down the road? While our faith does not require good works, our relationship with Jesus can grow when we become involved in his work.

Think about this: if your neighbor is someone you almost never talk to, you will not feel much strife if one day he dies. But if you have worked side by side with him for years; if you've shared tools, helped during tough times, and been a friend, his death will come hard for you. That is because you are emotionally invested in your neighbor.

We need to also be emotionally invested in Christ. He has given us gifts and skills, but we need to use them for him. Whether we focus these gifts through our church or find other ways to serve, our work will make our relationship with him grow. God did not provide these gifts to only use once; he wants you to use them every day.

A Message from the Fields

Luke 2:8–20

[8]And there were shepherds living out in the fields nearby, keeping watch over their flocks at night. [9]An angel of the Lord appeared to them, and the glory of the Lord shone around them, and they were terrified. [10]But the angel said to them, "Do not be afraid. I bring you good news that will cause great joy for all the people. [11]Today in the town of David a Savior has been born to you; he is the Messiah, the Lord. [12]This will be a sign to you: You will find a baby wrapped in cloths and lying in a manger."

[13]Suddenly a great company of the heavenly host appeared with the angel, praising God and saying,

[14]"Glory to God in the highest heaven,

and on earth peace to those on whom his favor rests."

[15]When the angels had left them and gone into heaven, the shepherds said to one another, "Let's go to Bethlehem and see this thing that has happened, which the Lord has told us about."

[16]So they hurried off and found Mary and Joseph, and the baby, who was lying in the manger. [17]When they had seen him, they spread the word concerning what had been told them about this child, [18]and all who heard it were amazed at what the shepherds said to them. [19]But Mary treasured up all these things and pondered them in her heart. [20]The shepherds returned, glorifying and praising God for all the things they had heard and seen, which were just as they had been told.

THINK OF ONE of those late nights when you are still doing fieldwork well after dark, milking cows before the morning breaks, or hunting down cattle to bring back for a morning shipment. It is quiet and peaceful, and you feel like you are all alone. Suddenly, you are surrounded by a great light and singing. You realize right away that you are surrounded by angels, even though you have never seen an angel before. Then one of the angels tells you to go into town and see a baby that has been placed in a manger. That baby, the angel tells you, is going to be the savior of the world.

I have had some weird nights before, but I think singing angels with a message would by far top any of my nights. Why would angels come singing to me? Now, I know that farmers can be important and do great things, but why did the angels come to me? Why didn't they go to the editor of the paper? Why didn't they go to the county council or the mayor? Maybe these angels are just making the rounds to everyone and they finally made their way out to the country. That's probably why they were mistaken and said that the baby was in a manger. They must be tired too. No one in their right mind would keep a new baby in the barn. Yes, they must be mistaken.

The shepherds witnessed an amazing thing when Jesus was born. I may be a little proud, but I think it is pretty cool that God chose to tell a bunch of farmers and herdsmen about the birth of his son before anyone else. He could have chosen to find a king, someone wealthy, or even the heralds. But he chose a bunch of guys who had been living in the hills nearby.

Think of how dirty and smelly you are sometimes when you get home from work. Now think of the shepherds, who had probably been out in the fields for at least a few days. Imagine the look on Mary's face when this group of men came bursting through the door to see her baby Jesus.

God did not choose the shepherds because of their social status; he chose them for just being themselves. From the very beginning he showed the world that he would love every group of people regardless of who they were or where they had come from. The people simply needed to accept him as their savior. When the shepherds arrived, they bowed down and worshiped him. Would a king have done the same?

God sent the shepherds to tell everyone about Jesus. These atypical messengers were average guys who were suddenly given a big job. They did not underestimate their role. Today we still have the job of telling others about Jesus. We probably will not get angels singing to us from the sky, but more than two thousand years later there are still people who need to hear the good news of Jesus. If a bunch of unwashed shepherds could tell the world, then so can you.

Take a Helping Hand

Philippians 2:19–24

[19]I hope in the Lord Jesus to send Timothy to you soon, that I also may be cheered when I receive news about you. [20]I have no one else like him, who will show genuine concern for your welfare. [21]For everyone looks out for their own interests, not those of Jesus Christ. [22]But you know that Timothy has proved himself, because as a son with his father he has served with me in the work of the gospel. [23]I hope, therefore, to send him as soon as I see how things go with me. [24]And I am confident in the Lord that I myself will come soon.

DO YOU HAVE THE BENEFIT of others helping you on your farm, or does everything rely on you? If you have help, it is probably because in your busy days there is simply not time to get everything done. As the saying goes, "there are not enough hours in the day."

Those who help you might be grouped into several categories. Maybe they are family, such as your spouse, children, parents, in-laws, nieces and nephews, or even grandchildren. Other times we go outside the family ties and receive help from neighbors, friends, and other farmers. Some employees may be hired based on their qualifications, or they may be the only people willing to do your work for what you can afford to pay.

While some farmers can do everything alone, most of us need help to some degree. We do not have to be superheroes and do everything ourselves. Look at some of the famous people in the Bible. Laban hired his nephew Jacob to help manage his flocks in Genesis. Moses needed help from his brother Aaron to lead the Israelites out of Egypt. Even Jesus knew he needed help, so he called the twelve disciples.

Sometimes we want to do it all alone, but we need help. If Jesus, who could calm a storm and raise the dead, needed help, then it is not wrong for us to get help too. While we may like to work day in and day out, even Jesus took time to rest, pray, and be with God. Those helpers can make sure we do that too.

Once we have the help, we need to trust them. Paul had Timothy to help him. In the book of Philippians, we see that Paul had built up a good relationship with the people of Philippi. However, as we know from Paul's other letters, he had also built up relationships with many other churches. They all had their strengths and weaknesses, but frankly they still needed help from Paul. With the speed of travel at this time in history, even physically getting to all these churches would be a challenge for Paul.

Paul trusted Timothy. He did not say, "Well, I know Timothy does great work but I really think I should be the one to do this because I helped start this church." Paul recognized that he could not do everything and that he would not be there forever.

Paul used Timothy and other early Christians to help the church grow. Through these helpers, the church was able to grow far faster and stronger than it ever would have if Paul had tried to manage everything by himself.

Do you trust those who work for you? Are you missing out on growth and success because you will not give up any control? Whether it is a child or a hired hand, your workers need your guidance, not your complete control, to grow. Sure, they will make mistakes, but that is how we learn. Let those mistakes grow their skills, and you may find that your life has a little less stress.

Fact or Fiction: Good Works Save

Matthew 25:37–40

[37]"Then the righteous will answer him, 'Lord, when did we see you hungry and feed you, or thirsty and give you something to drink? [38]When did we see you a stranger and invite you in, or needing clothes and clothe you? [39]When did we see you sick or in prison and go to visit you?'

[40]"The King will reply, 'Truly I tell you, whatever you did for one of the least of these brothers and sisters of mine, you did for me.'"

SERVING GOD CAN BE CONFUSING. We know we are supposed to serve God and work toward his glory. Yet we also know that it is not our works that save us. No matter what we do, it is only by God's grace that we are able to enter heaven. We are completely helpless without his full control and free gift. In fact, if our sole reason for doing good is that we are trying to gain points with God to earn our salvation, then we are very wrong in our thinking.

Non-Christians often see this conundrum as a very odd thing about Christians. We say works do not earn us a place in heaven, but that nevertheless we should do good works. The key to the situation is this: we do good works because we want to serve God to build a relationship with him.

Here's an example. A farmer has two children: a senior in high school and a nine-year-old. Both are preparing to show an animal at the 4-H fair. The high school senior has been in 4-H for years, and this will be his last year showing. He has grown somewhat tired of all the work involved with preparing for the show and would much rather be feeding his father's entire herd than focusing on one cow. Nevertheless, he does the work because this is his last chance to become grand champion and he is determined to win.

On the other hand, the nine-year-old daughter is showing a sheep for the first time. She is excited about having her own animal to care for, and she dearly loves her sheep. Every day she spends hours with it, walking it, feeding it, and even sitting and talking to it. It may very well be her best friend.

Both animals receive the same care. They both get trained, fed, and groomed. But the young girl has a relationship with her sheep. Even though she is doing chores to take care of it, she does the chores because she loves it. Her brother, on the other hand, cares for his cow simply because that is what needs to be done.

Serving God builds our relationship with him. Just as the little girl would never get attached to her sheep if she did not spend time with it doing the dirty work, we cannot get close to God without serving him. But if we are serving with the wrong attitude, our relationship is not growing because we are expecting something in return. If we work to build a relationship with God, God will bless us because he always loves us.

The Festival of Harvest

Exodus 23:16–19

[16]"Celebrate the Festival of Harvest with the firstfruits of the crops you sow in your field.

"Celebrate the Festival of Ingathering at the end of the year, when you gather in your crops from the field.

[17]"Three times a year all the men are to appear before the Sovereign LORD.

[18]"Do not offer the blood of a sacrifice to me along with anything containing yeast.

"The fat of my festival offerings must not be kept until morning.

[19]"Bring the best of the firstfruits of your soil to the house of the LORD your God.

"Do not cook a young goat in its mother's milk.

HOW DO YOU CELEBRATE the Festival of the Harvest? I am assuming you will have a party. What is your family doing for the Festival of Ingathering this year? Will you be traveling to your in-laws again?

Reading Exodus in the twenty-first century, it can seem a little archaic. It talks about traditions and practices that simply are not practiced or do not need to be practiced anymore. When we sin today, we do not get forgiveness by sacrificing an animal. We know that Jesus paid that final sacrifice for us and thus removed the need of a physical blood sacrifice to atone for our sins.

As we read Exodus today, it may almost seem silly to include some verses that talk about extinct traditions. It may seem more logical to just omit them from the Bible. But as we look at today's set of verses, we see some history of the people living in the Old Testament.

First, it is amazing to me that almost everyone must have been farmers to some degree, because God gave them specific instructions on how to offer their crops and animals as a sacrifice. While it was certainly a different age of farming, it can give us a feeling of connection to our very distant ancestry. They probably had sick animals, their crops died in floods, and they had animals run away. Yet God was faithful to them and loved them all the same. He helped them even when the times were tough.

God also asked the Israelites to love him. As they went through the harvest season, they celebrated the harvest and gave back to the Lord. Celebrating the harvest—does that sound a little like Thanksgiving? Yet when it is our turn to give back, do we take time to go to church and give thanks, or do turkey, family, and football get in the way?

When we give our gifts to God, he wants us to do it out of love rather than out of obligation. I think that is what makes our gifts amazing compared to the stringent rules of the Old Testament sacrifices. We have so many opportunities to express our love to God, and as long as we do it with the right intentions it will be a sacrifice of love to him.

So, remember to give back to God. Whether they include money, possessions, or even our valuable time, gifts to God are pleasing when they come from our hearts.

Age Discrimination

1 Samuel 16:7–13

[7]But the LORD said to Samuel, "Do not consider his appearance or his height, for I have rejected him. The LORD does not look at the things people look at. People look at the outward appearance, but the LORD looks at the heart."

[8]Then Jesse called Abinadab and had him pass in front of Samuel. But Samuel said, "The LORD has not chosen this one either." [9]Jesse then had Shammah pass by, but Samuel said, "Nor has the LORD chosen this one." [10]Jesse had seven of his sons pass before Samuel, but Samuel said to him, "The LORD has not chosen these." [11]So he asked Jesse, "Are these all the sons you have?"

"There is still the youngest," Jesse answered. "He is tending the sheep."

Samuel said, "Send for him; we will not sit down until he arrives."

[12]So he sent for him and had him brought in. He was glowing with health and had a fine appearance and handsome features.

Then the LORD said, "Rise and anoint him; this is the one."

[13]So Samuel took the horn of oil and anointed him in the presence of his brothers, and from that day on the Spirit of the LORD came powerfully upon David. Samuel then went to Ramah.

HAVE YOU EVER BEEN TOLD you could not do something because you were not tall enough, strong enough, or smart enough? As a child, this can be disappointing, but sometimes as an adult it is downright embarrassing. We know what our own capabilities are, but when others look down at us, it can be frustrating.

I started my first business when I was fifteen years old. I was working as a consultant for a few farms in different parts of the country. For my first few years, I worked hard to keep my age secret, while trying to provide top-notch service. Since most of my work was phone and Internet based, I was able to do this. By the time I was in college, I had a well-established business, and I did less to hide my age. It was sometimes frustrating, though, that after six-plus years in the business some people would still not take me seriously because I was younger than them.

David was a victim of age discrimination. When Samuel came to Jesse's house to anoint the next king, his father considered all his brothers first. Since all the brothers were parading before Samuel, little David had to stay out in the pasture to tend the sheep. But God was not going to anoint based on size, age, or experience. God looked at their hearts and chose David. David would go on to kill a giant as a boy, and one day he would become king.

If you are a young person today, I encourage you to not let your youth be an excuse to limit your success. Whether you take leadership on your farm or elsewhere, you have the opportunity to grow through doing. Let responsibility build your life.

We all choose not to do certain things because of our limitations. Sometimes as Christians we let our supposed lack of spiritual knowledge convince us that we are not strong in faith. We may be afraid to teach a Sunday school class or attend a Bible study because we are not good enough in our faith. However, God does not look at physical appearance or the depth of our spiritual knowledge; he looks at the heart. With even a tiny bit of faith, you have the opportunity to do great things. Let God be the power behind that faith as you grow throughout your life.

But God, I Want It My Way!

Exodus 17:1–6

¹The whole Israelite community set out from the Desert of Sin, traveling from place to place as the LORD commanded. They camped at Rephidim, but there was no water for the people to drink. ²So they quarreled with Moses and said, "Give us water to drink."

Moses replied, "Why do you quarrel with me? Why do you put the LORD to the test?"

³But the people were thirsty for water there, and they grumbled against Moses. They said, "Why did you bring us up out of Egypt to make us and our children and livestock die of thirst?"

⁴Then Moses cried out to the LORD, "What am I to do with these people? They are almost ready to stone me."

⁵The LORD answered Moses, "Go out in front of the people. Take with you some of the elders of Israel and take in your hand the staff with which you struck the Nile, and go. ⁶I will stand there before you by the rock at Horeb. Strike the rock, and water will come out of it for the people to drink." So Moses did this in the sight of the elders of Israel.

GIVE ME, GIVE ME, GIVE ME! This problem is all too common in society. If we do not have something, we should just demand it from someone else. Many social programs in the United States have become the norm for some individuals instead of the temporary helping hand they were intended to be. Fraud in social security, disability, and unemployment programs runs rampant while those who truly need the assistance suffer. Some who lose their jobs prefer to spend their days protesting against corporations rather than searching for a new job or working to improve their situation.

Moses had to deal with a group of complainers too. The Israelites had just been rescued through Moses by God from four hundred years of slavery in Egypt. You'd think the Israelites would have been happy to be out of this bondage. However, they did not fully understand the greatness of the Promised Land to come. Instead, they were only focused on the moment—they simply wanted to complain.

God remained faithful to his people as he led them through the desert. He gave them a pillar of fire and a cloud to lead them. He gave them manna and quail to eat. Nevertheless, they still doubted him. They complained to Moses so much that they were ready to kill him. They acted like they should be in control, but forgot that God was their provider.

We can sometimes act like the Israelites in the desert. As Christians we are freed from sin, but we sometimes forget about our Promised Land of heaven. As we continue through the desert of life, we can forget about the greatness of God and his providing.

We all deal with daily problems. A drought may make us wish for Moses' staff. We deal with farm problems such as escaped animals, broken equipment, and bad weather. Our relationship with our family may not always be what we want it to be. It can be easy to forget about God or even blame him during tough times.

When times are tough, it is important to remember that God is there, and he will support us. Sometimes that means he will fix our problems; other times, he will give us the strength to deal with them. But ultimately, we know the problems of earth are minor compared to the greatness of heaven.

The next time the tractor breaks, you get kicked by your livestock, or you are simply frustrated by a bad day, pause for a moment and ask God for help and strength. A few minutes with him may very well change your attitude for the rest of the day.

Reaching Out and Letting In

Ezekiel 34:1–6

[1]The word of the LORD came to me: [2]"Son of man, prophesy against the shepherds of Israel; prophesy and say to them: 'This is what the Sovereign LORD says: Woe to the shepherds of Israel who only take care of themselves! Should not shepherds take care of the flock? [3]You eat the curds, clothe yourselves with the wool and slaughter the choice animals, but you do not take care of the flock. [4]You have not strengthened the weak or healed the sick or bound up the injured. You have not brought back the strays or searched for the lost. You have ruled them harshly and brutally. [5]So they were scattered because there was no shepherd, and when they were scattered they became food for all the wild animals. [6]My sheep wandered over all the mountains and on every high hill. They were scattered over the whole earth, and no one searched or looked for them.'"

IF YOUR FARM HAS ANIMALS, you know how important it is to care for *all* the animals: the weak, strong, young, and old. They are all livestock, and they all contribute to the success of your farm. The strongest and best need care because they will benefit you the most. But the weak also need care so they can grow stronger and healthier. Plus, they are already a part of your farm and simply not caring for them would lower their value to nothing. If an animal dies it becomes worthless, but even a low-quality animal can still be sold for certain uses. Favoritism is not practical on a farm.

Unfortunately, some churches today show favoritism. Sometimes this is intentional, but sometimes the churches do it without realizing. Members may be well cared for in a church, but the church is blind to the community and the world around it. As a result, visitors never make it into the church, and the story of God is kept a secret within the church.

In other cases, certain people are rejected from the church all together. It can seem hard to believe that a church could be so harsh, but it can happen without us even realizing it. Think of what would happen if a known prostitute came into church on Sunday and sat down in the pew next to you. We may not intend to be harsh, but our reflexes may cause us to shy away from someone who is truly searching for God at that moment and needs all the support she can get.

Churches can also get wrapped up in their own traditions. Hymnals, worship folders, constant standing and sitting, and offering plates can all seem frightening to a visitor. While all these are done for valid reasons and with good intentions, a visitor to your church may be quickly overwhelmed and not return without some guidance and love from the members.

So, what can we as individuals do? First, get involved with people from a variety of backgrounds in your daily life. If you do not know who the sick, hungry, and injured are, find ways to reach out to them. Chances are there is great need in your community, but it does not always come knocking on your door.

Second, be a warm face to anyone who may visit your church. Welcoming visitors is not just the job of the pastor, ushers, and greeters. Introduce yourself, ask the other person for his or her name, and invite the person to join you again for worship. Try to develop a relationship with regular visitors. Showing interest goes a long way with someone who is experiencing a church for the first time.

Finally, continue to go into the world. God says in Ezekiel that his sheep are scattered over the whole earth. If God is calling you beyond your community, consider what he wants, even though it may seem like the last thing on your mind. Paul reminds us that we can do great things through Christ who gives us strength.

Break Time

Matthew 8:18–22

[18]When Jesus saw the crowd around him, he gave orders to cross to the other side of the lake. [19]Then a teacher of the law came to him and said, "Teacher, I will follow you wherever you go."

[20]Jesus replied, "Foxes have dens and birds have nests, but the Son of Man has no place to lay his head."

[21]Another disciple said to him, "Lord, first let me go and bury my father."

[22]But Jesus told him, "Follow me, and let the dead bury their own dead."

DO YOU EVER FEEL like you are really busy each day as a farmer? Farming often does not follow a nine-to-five schedule. Sometimes days off or vacations far from home are not really an option. But time is one of the many sacrifices farmers make to do their jobs. It may not always be easy, but we do what we do because it is what needs to be done.

In Matthew 8, Jesus explained some of the challenges he and his disciples were facing. While following Jesus and being a disciple certainly had some perks, it also had to wear on the disciples physically and emotionally. Jesus explained to one person the difficulty of traveling. Even the animals had a place to call home, but once Jesus started his ministry he was essentially a wanderer. He did not have a house or even a hometown any more. When he tried to visit Nazareth, he was run out of town.

Another person was told that by following Jesus he would miss out on some of his family events. Following Jesus would not be easy, but it would be important. Would these early followers be up to it? The twelve disciples certainly had made some sacrifices.

Even today, Christians do not always have smooth sailing. We still experience hardships. There can be persecution because of our faith. Sometimes fighting sin and temptation can be overwhelming. Even the church can suffer from infighting. Challenges surround us.

Fortunately, just as Jesus was there to support the early followers, God is with us today. Even Jesus took time out of his busy schedule to spend time with his Father. God gives us strength in the tough times, and celebrates the good with us.

We know as farmers we have lots of work ahead of us each year, and we know there will be plenty of challenges that we wish we could avoid. Nevertheless, we continue to farm each year, and we do our job, ready to conquer these challenges. As we go into our Christian life, we need to remember that we will have to make sacrifices as Christians. But, with God's backing, we can face those challenges head on and continue to grow in our faith.

Pasture or Feedlot?

Ezekiel 34:14–16

[14]I will tend them in a good pasture, and the mountain heights of Israel will be their grazing land. There they will lie down in good grazing land, and there they will feed in a rich pasture on the mountains of Israel. [15]I myself will tend my sheep and have them lie down, declares the Sovereign LORD. [16]I will search for the lost and bring back the strays. I will bind up the injured and strengthen the weak, but the sleek and the strong I will destroy. I will shepherd the flock with justice.

DO YOU KNOW all your livestock by name? Sure, you may be able to recognize each animal if your herd is not too large, but it is not common to see a farmer give personal names to animals in the twenty-first century. Rightly or wrongly, farmers have slowly separated themselves from their animals over the years.

If we look at Biblical times, livestock owners relied on a shepherd to manage the flocks. The feed lots and freestall barns of today did not exist. The livestock were mostly left to roam in the hills. However, the animals were not simply turned loose. They had the shepherds to watch over and care for them. The shepherds spent days at a time living with the livestock, protecting them from wild animals, finding fresh ground, and keeping any sheep from wandering off. Because they spent so much time with their sheep, they had personal connections with the animals. A good shepherd had a strong love for his flock.

We do not see this type of commitment very often today in confined livestock operations. The animals are confined to a fenced-in area, feed is delivered at set intervals, and other care is provided as needed. The animals are very well managed and cared for, but with more efficiency come larger flocks. With larger flocks comes a less personal connection. The farmer still cares for his animals, but it is a different degree of care than that a shepherd provided in the Bible. I'm not suggesting this is wrong; I'm simply noting that things have changed.

Throughout the Bible, Jesus and God are described as shepherds caring for their flocks. I think it would be interesting to see if God would use this metaphor with today's farming models. God does not throw us into a small, protected pen where we are immune from all daily struggle and danger like animals in a feedlot. Instead, we are let out into the pasture. However, we are not left to fend for ourselves.

Jesus is our shepherd and he watches all of us. When danger comes, he helps protect us and gives us the tools to ward it off. He helps provide for us in body and soul by giving us jobs, food, and fellow Christians to support our spiritual life. When we wander off, Jesus searches for us and asks us to come back to him. But he gives us the freedom to make these decisions on our own.

Why does he do all this? He does it because he knows our names and he loves each of us as individuals. If we tended a flock of billions, we certainly would not be able to show any degree of care to each individual. Jesus, however, knows each person's name and so much more! He loves everyone and wants them to come to him. He is our guide and our strength in all that we do.

If Only . . .

Philippians 4:11–13

[11]I am not saying this because I am in need, for I have learned to be content whatever the circumstances. [12]I know what it is to be in need, and I know what it is to have plenty. I have learned the secret of being content in any and every situation, whether well fed or hungry, whether living in plenty or in want. [13]I can do all this through him who gives me strength.

IF ONLY WE WOULD GET a little more rain. If only I could afford a little larger tractor. If only we could plant a little more land this year. If only commodity prices were just a little higher. If only . . .

Do you ever feel like your goals are just out of reach? You may feel like you are doing fairly well, but adding just a little more would make life great. Maybe your family is getting by, but it would sure be nice to have just a little bit more so you could give them a nice treat. Maybe then you could get that new toy or take a little more time off.

The problem is that as humans we are never satisfied: when we achieve something, we want more. It could be for a variety of reasons, such as the pressures of successful neighbors who push us. Sometimes it may not even be greed that pushes us. We may view success as an ultimatum. In other words, if you have a good, profitable year that means that you must take that profit and invest in more land or livestock. We assume that success must equal growth.

On the flip side, bad times can come too. As farmers, chances are good that at some point—or quite often—we will face challenges that are less than desirable. When this happens, it is easy to become complainers and whine about our current situation. We worry about what will happen to our farm and family. While providing for family needs should be a priority, it can easily consume us so that we may be angry with family members when we do not achieve, and it hurts our relationship with them.

As a part of my business, I work with farmers in different parts of the country who come from very different backgrounds. As important as it is to stay in contact, sometimes I hate making small talk with them about the current situation on their farm. A simple "How are you doing?" can quickly turn into a rant about how horribly things are going at the farm. First, I should say that I do not mind listening to problems and struggles; that is part of my job and is an important part of what I do to understand my customers' needs. However, I have noticed that complaining becomes a habit with certain people. Over the years, I have rarely if ever had a discussion with them where things are good. After a while, I began to realize that no matter what happens their outlook is pessimistic. I still certainly enjoy working with these farmers, but I feel some pain for their sake that pessimism is dragging them down.

Constant pessimism can be dangerous. We know as farmers and as humans that there are going to be low points in our lives. However, self-pity will get us nowhere. When we can be content in every situation, we will live a much happier life.

We are rarely on the point of complete collapse, so take joy in the small things. When drought is drying up the crops, take joy that your livestock will bring in some income. When your tractor breaks down, take joy in the fact that you have a tractor in the first place. When the cows break a fence and get out, be thankful you have cows, are able to find them all, that you have people to help you find them, or that fences were invented so that you do not have to go on a hunt every day to find your livestock. Sometimes it is not easy to find the little things to be thankful for, but your outlook can change everything.

The next time you feel overwhelmed with problems, stop and give thanks to God for the small blessings you have. God will be our strength, and if you invite him along in the struggles he will help you through them. When God helps me keep my attitude in check, a bad day can end up not so bad after all. Certainly the problems are still there, but even a small smile makes my day go a little better.

Bad Days

Job 39:5–12

⁵"Who let the wild donkey go free?
Who untied his ropes?
⁶I gave him the wasteland as his home,
the salt flats as his habitat.
⁷He laughs at the commotion in the town;
he does not hear a driver's shout.
⁸He ranges the hills for his pasture
and searches for any green thing.

⁹"Will the wild ox consent to serve you?
Will he stay by your manger at night?
¹⁰Can you hold him to the furrow with a harness?
Will he till the valleys behind you?
¹¹Will you rely on him for his great strength?
Will you leave your heavy work to him?
¹²Can you trust him to bring in your grain
and gather it to your threshing floor?"

ONE JOB WAS PARTICULARLY frustrating a few summers ago on our farm. We were upgrading our irrigation system, and we buried lots of new pipe underground. When we were finished, we tested the system and everything worked fine. After some dry weather in early June we finally started the system to use it. It ran great for the first five minutes. But suddenly, the water stopped flowing.

Two sections of new pipe had split apart underground. We dug them up, fixed the break, poured some concrete around it, and let it sit overnight. The next day we started it up, but had the same results. After wasting two days of work and a lot more concrete than we should have needed, we finally thought the broken section would hold. It did. Unfortunately, the pipe burst at another point under the pressure.

We went back to work and fixed the new hole. Our system finally started working and we watered until the next rain a few days later. A week later one of our employees backed into one of the risers coming out of the ground. There did not seem to be any damage, and we did a quick test. There seemed to be no problems. However, two weeks later when we needed the system and started it back up, the pipe began to leak at the riser.

We dug another hole, welded the riser, and started the system. The pipe shot another hole on the other side of the riser, so we dug it out and replaced it. Unfortunately, the new riser was defective and leaked too. Desperate for water, and tired of fixing irrigation problems, we had the irrigation company replace the broken piece. The replacement piece was also defective. Finally, after one more fix and nearly ten repairs, our irrigation system was in working condition.

As farmers, sometimes it is easy to become frustrated with the many challenges we face, especially when we are out of control. We can try to control the weather by irrigating, putting up wind breaks, or using frost protection, but the weather still destroys crops. We can try to feed our animals perfect rations, provide proper care, and give regular vaccinations and veterinary checks, but they still can get sick or die. We can run our farm perfectly, but at the end of the year we may not always make a profit, for a variety of reasons.

In the book of Job, God had to remind Job who was in control. Job started to question God about why all sorts of bad things happened to him. God came right back and asked Job how powerful Job thought he was. God pointed out to Job that everything on earth happens because of God.

Sometimes we feel like we are in control. Technology gives us this confidence. Humans have created chemicals that kill troublesome plants. Humans have learned how to breed animals and artificially inseminate them. Humans have created equipment to do almost any task. Yet we have this power because God gave us knowledge. He created the raw materials that make these technologies possible. He controls the world that allows these technologies to continue to exist.

Throughout our struggles with the broken irrigation, it was easy to get frustrated, imagining that our crops would die from lack of water. I probably did not fully rely on the knowledge that God would provide. However, even if our crops had died, God would have used that problem to improve his world, though I may not have understood how.

It is not wrong to use technology that God has blessed us with. I believe that God gave us irrigation to use his resources better. At the end of the day, though, it is our job to remember that he created every gift of this earth.

In My Father's Barn, There Are Many Stalls

John 14:1–4

[1]"Do not let your hearts be troubled. You believe in God; believe also in me. [2]My Father's house has many rooms; if that were not so, would I have told you that I am going there to prepare a place for you? [3]And if I go and prepare a place for you, I will come back and take you to be with me that you also may be where I am. [4]You know the way to the place where I am going."

A FEW YEARS AGO, a large family dairy farm nearby was adding a new freestall barn and expanding capacity to house an extra five hundred cows. The construction was almost complete, and they were only a few weeks away from moving in some new cows. Then, in the middle of the night, one of the owners received a call from a stranger.

The stranger apologized for the late-night call, and explained that he had a dairy farm about fifty miles south, in the next state. He had just received lots of rain, and a river ran right next to his farm. The river kept rising, and the farmer was worried. Not only was his family in danger, but his three-hundred-head dairy herd was also in danger of being washed away. A few neighbors had offered to help house some cows, but none could take more than ten or fifteen animals.

The farmer who had just been awoken knew what had to be done. He told the farmer not to worry, and to start preparing his animals to leave the farm. Some trucks would arrive shortly. The sleepy farmer called up his family, employees, and friends, and started immediately organizing the transport of three hundred cows across state lines to safety. While a few people headed in trucks to start moving cows, others stayed at the farm and made last-minute changes to prepare for the unexpected guests. Makeshift gates were constructed, feed was quickly moved in, and unload ramps were set in place. By six in the morning his empty barn was full of cows lining up to head to the parlor to be milked. Every last cow was milked on time.

I have never met either of those farmers, and I recount this story only from my memory of the newspaper story I read. I can only imagine the gratitude that farmer in trouble felt. He had been watching the water get closer for days. He had probably hoped the water would stop rising, but it did not. He tried to find other options, but there were none. There were no options until someone gave him the name of a stranger.

Can you imagine his face when he showed up with the last load at a farm miles from home and saw his cows were already eating and lining up to be milked? Can you imagine what went through his mind as he saw complete strangers moving his cattle and caring for them? They had no idea if he could pay them back, if this new farmer was a good person, if his animals were well cared for, or why he had not decided at noon instead of midnight to ask for help.

For each of us, there will come a time when we will be completely helpless. It is called death. Death can be a scary thought for a lot of people. What lies beyond the grave? For a non-Christian, this can be a topic of great uncertainty. As Christians, we know there are two options: heaven or hell. We know the latter to be eternally awful.

We also know that God gives us the offer of heaven. He tells us there are plenty of rooms. His freestall barn has room for everyone. He has gone there to prepare everything for us. We do not have to worry about whether there will be room for us or what we will eat or wear. God has prepared a gift of generosity beyond comprehension. He promises to take us there if we believe in him and trust in his promise.

God blesses us on earth even though we sometimes have struggles. It is a great comfort to us in every struggle to know that the best blessing is still to come.

The Shepherd's Voice

John 10:1–10

[1]"Very truly I tell you Pharisees, anyone who does not enter the sheep pen by the gate, but climbs in by some other way, is a thief and a robber. [2]The one who enters by the gate is the shepherd of the sheep. [3]The gatekeeper opens the gate for him, and the sheep listen to his voice. He calls his own sheep by name and leads them out. [4]When he has brought out all his own, he goes on ahead of them, and his sheep follow him because they know his voice. [5]But they will never follow a stranger; in fact, they will run away from him because they do not recognize a stranger's voice." [6]Jesus used this figure of speech, but the Pharisees did not understand what he was telling them.

[7]Therefore Jesus said again, "Very truly I tell you, I am the gate for the sheep. [8]All who have come before me are thieves and robbers, but the sheep have not listened to them. [9] I am the gate; whoever enters through me will be saved. They will come in and go out, and find pasture. [10]The thief comes only to steal and kill and destroy; I have come that they may have life, and have it to the full."

I MUST ADMIT that I am not much of an animal handler. I have never had the knack of calming an animal or commanding it to take action. Those who can train animals are good at what they do. Many livestock may not be the brightest creatures. But most know if someone or something is kind or mean. When they see their caretaker or trainer, they behave differently.

As a child, I would watch my dad milk cows. Moving among them, he would gently touch their backs as he got close so he would not startle them. As he moved between two of them, he bent down, trusting that they would not kick him. They stayed calm as he carefully washed their udders and put on the milking machine. They trusted him.

Then there was me. Maybe I was a little skittish because I was young, but it seemed like every time I got near the cows, they would jump and move about. They never seemed to like me. The only thing I was good at was moving them all out of the barn: they just wanted to get away from me.

Jesus often compares himself to a shepherd and people to his flock. In John 10, Jesus criticizes the Pharisees who are the leaders in the temple. He tells them that they are not serving God and his people as they should. Elsewhere, Jesus becomes so mad at the corruption in the temple that he overturns the tables of the merchants who sold things in the temple to offer as sacrifices. He was teaching the people that they were being misled by the corruption of the Pharisees.

The Pharisees knew Jesus was different and they hated him. People were following Jesus in large numbers, and they felt threatened. Why were these people turning from following the commands of the Pharisees to following the teachings of this man who was not even a priest? Jesus tells them that his people know him and they follow him. They recognize his voice and want to learn from him. However, the Pharisees would rather have listened to their own ideas and the worldly views than to the teaching of God's only son.

Whose voice do you listen to today? Do you feel comforted and strengthened by the teaching of Jesus? Or would you rather follow the corruption of this world? It can be really easy to choose the wrong route. The thieves and robbers can promise greener pastures and a better life outside the confines of following Jesus. But when we get out into the world, we see that it is not all that we imagined. Adam and Eve experienced this when they chose not to follow God's command.

The world can do bad things to us, but God promises life. When we step away from evil, we can see the great benefits of a life with God. The thieves of this world will continue to tempt us until the day we die, but Jesus is our shepherd and his voice will call us every day.

Hunger Pains

John 6:35, 40

[35]Then Jesus declared, "I am the bread of life. Whoever comes to me will never go hungry, and whoever believes in me will never be thirsty . . . [40]For my Father's will is that everyone who looks to the Son and believes in him shall have eternal life, and I will raise them up at the last day."

DO YOU EVER GET those days when no matter what you eat you are still hungry? For me, it usually happens in spells of a few days. I usually eat breakfast early in the morning, around five or five-thirty. By nine-thirty, I am a long way from lunch but I am already getting really hungry. I crave food, so I find a quick snack. Yet it seems like ten minutes later I am still hungry.

The thing I will never understand about my stomach is that if for some reason I miss breakfast, I usually am not any hungrier at nine-thirty than when I ate breakfast. So where does my breakfast go? Why do I feel hungry?

Jesus tells us that he is the bread of life. He tells us that by believing in him we will not be hungry or thirsty. Now that sounds like a pretty good deal. Pack up the kids and head to church, and we can all get free food, right? Obviously Jesus is using a spiritual metaphor, but what does the bread of life really mean to us as Christians?

We all need food and water to survive. Cut off the supply for even a few days, and we will be in trouble. This is just like our relationship with Jesus. It needs constant care. If we decided that we were only going to eat and drink on Sundays, we would struggle to stay alive. Likewise, going to church an hour each week is not going to build a strong relationship with Christ. We need to pray daily; study his word through devotions, Bible study, and other spiritual offerings; and we need to serve with the gifts God has given us.

You can feed your livestock daily, and they will grow and get stronger until they reach full maturity. Just like humans, they need food to exist. But God also made us special. He gave us souls. Humans are his chosen creatures: we love, hate, learn, and have a relationship with him. If we choose to continually eat the spiritual food he provides to grow closer to him, we have the promise of heaven. Certainly it is not our actions that *earn* us heaven; God gives us that purely as a gift. But any choice to reject God removes the ability to receive that gift. Jesus tells us that God wants each of us to have eternal life in heaven with him. But instead of being like a newborn calf that refuses to drink the milk provided to us, we need to accept his gift and trust in him. It is only through our desire to have faith in God that we can be blessed by his gifts.

Unknown Blessings

Habakkuk 3:17–18

[17] Though the fig tree does not bud
    and there are no grapes on the vines,
though the olive crop fails
    and the fields produce no food,
though there are no sheep in the pen
    and no cattle in the stalls,
[18] yet I will rejoice in the LORD,
    I will be joyful in God my Savior.

ON OCCASION, you will be confronted with situations that you simply do not understand. Why was my farm destroyed by a storm? Why did that family member have to die? Why did that accident have to happen? No matter how much we question the problem, we cannot comprehend why it is happening. The good thing is that God knows what is happening too. He has a reason for everything that happens.

God does not always explain himself in ways that we as humans—with our limited insight and clouded vision—can always comprehend. So, instead of understanding every aspect of God's unfolding plan for our lives and our world, we must be satisfied to trust Him completely. Sometimes, a year later, we look back and say that everything now makes sense. Sometimes we never understand why certain events happen.

We cannot know God's motivations, nor can we understand his actions. We can, however, trust him, seek him, and obey him. As Christians, sometimes we need to let go of trying to understand everything around us. Sometimes we need to simply trust that God is in control and will help us through the tough times.

Acceptance means learning to trust God more. The prophet Habakkuk struggled with the concept of why bad things happened. As he worked to understand why, he came to realize that there is always a reason to praise God.

Today, think of at least one aspect of your life that you have been reluctant to accept, and then prayerfully ask God to help you trust Him more by accepting the past. Next, try to think about the many blessings you still have. Whether they are family, food, or possessions, I am willing to guess that you are still surrounded by many blessings. It can really hurt when sin destroys the blessings around us, especially when another person is involved. Yet God will continue to bless each of us every day with new blessings. Some days, your blessings will simply be having the ability to get out of bed on your own. This may not seem like a blessing, but ask many elderly people how easily they get out of bed, and you may have a new perspective.

The next time your olive crop or corn crop fails, lean on God in your struggle and continue to rejoice in your blessings.

The Element of Surprise

Matthew 24:42–44

42"Therefore keep watch, because you do not know on what day your Lord will come. 43But understand this: If the owner of the house had known at what time of night the thief was coming, he would have kept watch and would not have let his house be broken into. 44So you also must be ready, because the Son of Man will come at an hour when you do not expect him."

WHEN MY DAD was still milking cows, every six months or so the state milk inspector would come to our farm to make sure everything was being processed and cleaned correctly. The inspector had a long checklist to look over, and it always seemed like he or she would search until they found at least one thing to mark off. We were allowed to miss a certain number of points and still be in good standing, but too many marks and our farm could be in trouble.

The one thing my dad never liked about the milk inspectors was that they always showed up unannounced. They did this to make sure that the farms were following the rules every day. This meant that my father always needed to provide one hundred percent care and never take shortcuts. Even if one day it seemed easier to skip a step or take a shortcut, the threat of the milk inspector walking in at any moment kept everyone on their toes. In reality, it was not the bad reports themselves that kept the farmers in check, but simply the threat of a bad report.

Jesus tells us that there will be an element of surprise when he returns to earth too. We do not know the day or the hour. He could come at any time of any day. Tomorrow could be the day. Today could be the day. You may not even finish reading this devotion. Then again, Jesus may not come during your lifetime.

How do you react to knowing that Jesus may be here any day? Does it put any pressure on you? If he told you he would return in two weeks, I'm willing to bet you would live your next two weeks a little differently. Maybe you would spend more time praying or studying God's word. You might decide it is time to start witnessing to those around you to whom you were too timid to talk to before. You might start to ask for forgiveness from God and those around you. The problem is this: we simply do not know when Jesus will return.

Since we do not know the day or the hour, we have two options. First, we could live our days hoping that Jesus will wait a little longer and we will find time later to be more "godly." But no matter how you look at it, putting off Jesus until a later time is never a good idea.

The second option we have is to live every day for him. That does not mean we need to spend fourteen hours a day in church. We should, however, be praying, studying God's word, and sharing his love with those around us. If we live every day like it may be our last, we will be ready when he comes or our time ends. It will also make each of our days fulfilling. Just as a dairy farmer is always ready for his or her next inspection, we need to be ready for God's inspection.

If you are still not convinced, consider this: God knows everything you do, whether you like it or not. When he returns he is not going to look at the last thing you did. Instead, he will look at the whole person and see the love and humility you showed and the forgiveness you offered.

Thankful in Everything

Proverbs 27:23–27

²³Be sure you know the condition of your flocks,
 give careful attention to your herds;
²⁴for riches do not endure forever,
 and a crown is not secure for all generations.
²⁵When the hay is removed and new growth appears
 and the grass from the hills is gathered in,
²⁶the lambs will provide you with clothing,
 and the goats with the price of a field.
²⁷You will have plenty of goats' milk to feed your family
 and to nourish your female servants.

WHY DO WE WORK? As Christians with a great God, it can almost seem silly that we need to toil at all. We are told that God knows our names and cares for us. If that is the case, then as long as we trust God food should show up at our door and we should have a place to live every day. We should have no needs or worries.

Unfortunately, this simply is not true. God gave us skills, knowledge, and strength, and he expects us to use them. We are to put our hands to work to provide for ourselves and those around us. In Proverbs 27:23, the farmers of the Old Testament were told that simply having a flock of sheep would not make them successful or allow them to survive. They needed to care for the sheep too. If the flock was turned loose in the pasture, never to be cared for again, the sheep would wander off. They would not find water or new ground to graze. They would be attacked by wild animals or stolen by thieves.

We can agree that, even as Christians, our jobs and work are important. Yet in verse 24 we are reminded that being successful is not our ultimate goal. Our riches will one day end. When we die, what we have accumulated will stay here on earth and will be meaningless to us. Any power or position you gained will not carry over to heaven. So, while we need to work hard in our jobs, we need to keep the desire for wealth in check.

God offers many resources for us to provide for our families and live a life here on earth. Nice things are not necessarily a sin or bad to accumulate, but we need to remember who provides our blessings. If God wanted to, he could put obstacles in your way to prevent you from being successful. When we do have good times in our lives it is because God has richly blessed us.

We should give thanks to him for what he has done for us. This can be in prayer or by sharing those blessings with those around us. We can share by giving money to our churches or community programs. We can donate our time, which is a gift that every person is given. When we remember God after our blessings, it helps us keep our greed in check and put our hearts where they should be.

If it has been a while since you sat down and thanked God for all you have, take a few minutes today to do that. God is always listening, and he wants to hear from you.

God Is Speaking; Are You Listening?

Psalm 48:14

[14]For this God is our God for ever and ever;
he will be our guide even to the end.

GOD IS OUR GUIDE. Those are encouraging words, but when was the last time you came face to face with God? Has he walked into your barn recently just to visit? Has he ridden along with you in the tractor and talked about your concerns? Explaining our relationship with a God who we do not see in flesh and bone can be hard, especially if we are talking to someone who is not a Christian.

The exciting thing about our relationship with God is that he is able to speak to us without manifesting himself as flesh and bone. Sometimes he speaks to us through other people. Pastors, family members, friends, and even strangers may share something unexpected or something we need to hear. They may not know why they are concerned, where their wisdom is coming from, or even the full meaning of what they are speaking about. That is because God is working through them to speak to you. Other times God may put his thoughts directly in our minds. He may guide our thoughts or lead us to other ideas that may change our outlook of what we see or what we believe.

Sometimes God is knocking on our door and we simply choose to not answer. He guides our conscience, but we look the other way. He fills our minds with thoughts, but we choose to be distracted and find other things to think about. We may stray from church, which prevents a dose of God speaking to us through the pastors and other Christians.

I know there are times when God has been with me while on the farm. Numerous times, I should have been injured while working, but God has been there to carefully protect me. I have also done lots of thinking while riding on a tractor. I may pass the time with idle thoughts, but on more than one occasion God has pushed me to take action on something. I have no idea why these thoughts should have come to me, but as I look back I can see God was speaking to me. God works through our thoughts and leads us in ways we sometimes do not understand.

As you go about your day, keep an open mind. God may be speaking, but if you are not listening you will never hear him. If he does choose to speak to you, be ready to listen. Then pray. A good conversation always needs to go both ways, and this is certainly true with God. Ask for guidance concerning what he tells you, and pray for strength.

God is speaking; are you listening?

Impending Destruction

Isaiah 32:9–20

[9]You women who are so complacent,
rise up and listen to me;
you daughters who feel secure,
hear what I have to say!
[10]In little more than a year
you who feel secure will tremble;
the grape harvest will fail,
and the harvest of fruit will not come.
[11]Tremble, you complacent women;
shudder, you daughters who feel secure!
Strip off your clothes,
put sackcloth around your waists.
[12]Beat your breasts for the pleasant fields,
for the fruitful vines
[13]and for the land of my people,
a land overgrown with thorns and briers—
yes, mourn for all houses of merriment
and for this city of revelry.
[14]The fortress will be abandoned,
the noisy city deserted;
citadel and watchtower will become a wasteland forever,
the delight of donkeys, a pasture for flocks,
[15]till the Spirit is poured upon us from on high,
and the desert becomes a fertile field,
and the fertile field seems like a forest.
[16]Justice will dwell in the desert
and righteousness live in the fertile field.
[17]The fruit of righteousness will be peace;
the effect of righteousness will be quietness and confidence forever.

¹⁸My people will live in peaceful dwelling places,

in secure homes,

in undisturbed places of rest.

¹⁹Though hail flattens the forest

and the city is leveled completely,

²⁰how blessed you will be,

sowing your seed by every stream,

and letting your cattle and donkeys range free.

HAVE YOU EVER HAD the feeling that everything was about to come tumbling down? This passage from Isaiah is a warning that Isaiah gave to the people of Judah about the destruction that was coming. The city was under attack, and the crops and lands would be destroyed. Things were not going to be good for the people of Judah, and they could sense the impending terror.

In verse 16 the tone begins to change, and in verse 17 Isaiah says, "The fruit of righteousness will be peace." Even though there will be utter destruction, God's people will be safe. Verses 19 and 20 say, "Though hail flattens the forest, and the city is leveled completely, how blessed you will be, sowing your seed by every stream, and letting your cattle and donkeys range free." Does this mean that as Christians we will be protected from the evil of this world? Will our crops not suffer from weather, and will our animals always prosper? Unfortunately, as Christians we will suffer the same problems and challenges as the rest of the world.

I am glad that Christians will suffer too because I, like everyone else, have suffered my share of hardships from time to time. If I thought these problems came only because of a lack of faith, I would be in serious trouble. Life is not without challenges for Christ's followers, and we know we must face these obstacles.

There will come a time, though, when we will be exempt from the challenges, destruction, and pain on earth. That place is called heaven. The world will be destroyed, and everything in it. That will be an ugly day, but God will lead his followers to a greater place. We will have peaceful dwelling places, and we will still be blessed.

I do not know exactly what heaven will look like, but I know it is the place I want to be. God has promised and blessed us with so much, but the promise of heaven is by far the greatest promise I can ever imagine. We will be in God's presence for all eternity. We will be safe from the problems, illness, and evil of this world. Even as Jesus hung on the cross, he spoke of the promise of paradise. What a great promise that is for us all.

Great Treasure

Matthew 14:44–46

[44]"The kingdom of heaven is like treasure hidden in a field. When a man found it, he hid it again, and then in his joy went and sold all he had and bought that field.

[45]"Again, the kingdom of heaven is like a merchant looking for fine pearls. [46]When he found one of great value, he went away and sold everything he had and bought it."

HAVE YOU EVER HAD something that you wanted so badly that you would do almost anything to have it? Maybe it was a new truck, tickets to a big game, a restored tractor just like grandpa had when you were a kid, or a piece of land that came up for sale in the neighborhood. You know it will be expensive, but when you weigh the costs you know the expense will be worth it.

Every year when I watch the news on TV the day after Thanksgiving Black Friday shopping, I see millions of people who think they have found something of great value. Past reports have included people being trampled, pepper sprayed, and even shot as they rushed to get their great deal. Some of these people even give up being with family on Thanksgiving to make sure they hold their place in line. They do all of this to save $200 on a new TV.

Americans are avid consumers, and when we find something we want we work hard to get it. Part of the American Dream is that anyone can succeed if they only put their mind to it. Yet we still live in a country rife with homelessness, hunger, and evil.

Jesus tells two parables in Matthew 14 about our efforts to get to heaven. In both cases, the people in the stories sold everything they had to get their most valued possession. As a child I never understood the second parable. Why would a man sell his house and everything else he owned just to have a stinking pearl? Where would he live? How would he eat? While our situations may not be nearly as extreme, are the sacrifices we make for material things really worth it?

There is one sacrifice that *is* worth it, yet it is rarely a top priority: heaven. Think about it: if you had to get rid of every material possession in this world in order to go to heaven, would you do it? Would you abandon all your friends to go to heaven? Would you face daily mockery to go to heaven? You might not want to, but we are told that heaven is so great that we should do any of these things with gladness.

When was the last time you were genuinely excited about going to heaven? Are you more excited about heaven or about your upcoming vacation? While it is probably not necessary to get up and sell all of your possessions today, ask yourself what you are giving up for God. How does your sacrifice compare to giving up everything? Could you be giving back to God a little more?

Farming: Punishment and Blessing

Genesis 3:21–24

²¹The LORD God made garments of skin for Adam and his wife and clothed them. ²²And the LORD God said, "The man has now become like one of us, knowing good and evil. He must not be allowed to reach out his hand and take also from the tree of life and eat, and live forever." ²³So the LORD God banished him from the Garden of Eden to work the ground from which he had been taken. ²⁴After he drove the man out, he placed on the east side of the Garden of Eden cherubim and a flaming sword flashing back and forth to guard the way to the tree of life.

AS I CONSIDERED writing this book, I thought about how many times in the Bible farming stories or metaphors about farming were told. While there are a few exceptions, most of the stories make me feel good about farming. You do not see God telling too many stories about dentists, cooks, bus drivers, or politicians. It makes me feel privileged that God uses stories about farmers to teach his word. It is probably greedy and sinful to feel this pride, but it still makes me take notice.

Fortunately, to keep my ego in check God made sure to include some bad stories too. Today I am thinking about Genesis 3:21–24, when God kicked Adam and Eve out of the Garden of Eden. I did not even notice that this story was a reference to farming until today.

Verse 23 says, "So the LORD God banished him from the Garden of Eden to work the ground from which he had been taken." So what? God told Adam that he had to work the ground. We still do this today. Taken alone, this verse does not seem so bad.

We cannot forget, though, what happened just before this. Adam and Eve were living in paradise. They had plenty to eat, the world was perfect, and life was good. God would even stop by from time to time to hang out with them. They only had one rule, and yet they broke it. God was not happy. Adam and Eve would be punished for the sin they had committed.

In verse 23, we see that God is not saying, "Hey, I need some help taking care of the land around here, and since you are the only two people would you mind working it?" Unfortunately, this labor was not part of the paradise. This was the *punishment*. Being forced to live off the land was not going to be easy, but Adam and Eve had this coming because of the sin they committed. The fact that they were assigned their first career was not really a highlight for them.

Today, there are times when farming can feel like a punishment. We suffer in the heat, cold, rain, and drought. Our bodies get worked hard, and we sometimes feel worn down. Yet this is not a punishment reserved for farmers. All humans work to fill their needs daily. We all live with the effects of sin.

Despite the sin that caused this work, God still blesses us through our work. Farming also provides us opportunities to connect with God that many humans do not have the chance to experience. We are surrounded by the wonders of God's creation of land, animals, and plants. We do not sit in a glass office overlooking hundreds of other office buildings. We are given the important task of caring for God's creation. While God certainly could have chosen to care for his land and animals on his own, he wants us to have responsibility and to love what he has made. This is a responsibility that we should take seriously. In everything we do, we can farm for the Lord.

A Drought of Belief

1 Kings 17:1–6

[1]Now Elijah the Tishbite, from Tishbe in Gilead, said to Ahab, "As the LORD, the God of Israel, lives, whom I serve, there will be neither dew nor rain in the next few years except at my word."

[2]Then the word of the LORD came to Elijah: [3]"Leave here, turn eastward and hide in the Kerith Ravine, east of the Jordan. [4]You will drink from the brook, and I have directed the ravens to supply you with food there."

[5]So he did what the LORD had told him. He went to the Kerith Ravine, east of the Jordan, and stayed there. [6]The ravens brought him bread and meat in the morning and bread and meat in the evening, and he drank from the brook.

IMAGINE THAT YOUR pastor walked into your barn one day and said he had a message for you: because you refused to trust fully in God, it would not rain for the next few years. Until you repented and turned to God, your farm would not even see dew. That would be scary for any farmer.

Elijah's message to King Ahab was not the first time in the Bible that God withheld rain for years. Remember the seven years of famine in Egypt? King Ahab had completely rejected God and was worshiping false gods such as Baal. Ahab and his evil wife Jezebel had killed many of God's prophets who were trying to save the people of Israel.

Ahab knew the consequences of Elijah's announcement. The rivers would dry up and everything would die without any rain for years. Without thriving plants, there would be no food, and it would be hard to feed the livestock too. When even dry areas of our country go more than half a year with no rain, it can be tragic. Imagine the threat of years of drought. It is amazing how much we rely on water that we usually take for granted.

Despite knowing the challenges, Ahab watched Elijah walk away. Surely, Ahab thought, the God of Elijah had no control over the weather. He resisted believing in God, and we learn in 1 Kings 18 that Ahab even searched the land trying to find Elijah to kill him. He had been given many opportunities to know and trust God, but he always chose to reject him. Now his stubbornness was putting all the people of his kingdom at risk.

Ahab and his kingdom were about to come under great suffering, but God had a plan for Elijah. He took him to a remote area to hide during the drought. God sent ravens, certainly not the most glamorous animal, to provide for Elijah. All we know about his next year was that he stayed there. In a sense, God was giving him a time to rest, because God's plan took some time to execute.

It would have been hard for me to sit and wait. I can be an impatient person, and sitting in a canyon hiding while I waited for God to accomplish his goals would be hard. Yet God always has a plan. Sometimes we try to rush it, but that always ends badly. Other times God is asking us to take action, and we simply sit by waiting to be pushed.

In the next few sections we will look more closely at this story as it unfolds. But before we do so, think of this: how much drought would it have taken before you repented? I am certainly not saying that a drought today is a direct cause of specific sins. But if you were in Ahab's position, what would you change in your life to please God? Even though you are not being threatened with drought, what can you do to make some of those changes today?

Faith in an Empty Jar

1 Kings 17:7–16

[7]Some time later the brook dried up because there had been no rain in the land. [8]Then the word of the LORD came to him: [9]"Go at once to Zarephath in the region of Sidon and stay there. I have directed a widow there to supply you with food." [10]So he went to Zarephath. When he came to the town gate, a widow was there gathering sticks. He called to her and asked, "Would you bring me a little water in a jar so I may have a drink?" [11]As she was going to get it, he called, "And bring me, please, a piece of bread."

[12]"As surely as the LORD your God lives," she replied, "I don't have any bread—only a handful of flour in a jar and a little olive oil in a jug. I am gathering a few sticks to take home and make a meal for myself and my son, that we may eat it—and die."

[13]Elijah said to her, "Don't be afraid. Go home and do as you have said. But first make a small loaf of bread for me from what you have and bring it to me, and then make something for yourself and your son. [14]For this is what the LORD, the God of Israel, says: 'The jar of flour will not be used up and the jug of oil will not run dry until the day the LORD sends rain on the land.'"

[15]She went away and did as Elijah had told her. So there was food every day for Elijah and for the woman and her family. [16]For the jar of flour was not used up and the jug of oil did not run dry, in keeping with the word of the LORD spoken by Elijah.

AS WE CONTINUE the story about the drought, things were going well for Elijah. While the drought was severe, he had food provided by God through the ravens and water from a brook. One day, though, the brook dried up. As it kept getting lower and lower, Elijah may have sensed a little fear, wondering what would happen next. Yet we do not read about any unfaithfulness from him. Instead, when the water was gone God sent him into a different region.

As this story of Elijah continues, he encounters a widow preparing her last supper as her food supply has run out. Yet Elijah asks her to first make him a little food. He tells her that if she does this good deed, her flour will not run out. Elijah was a stranger, but despite the troubles she was going through, she took a servant's heart, trusted his word, and provided him with food. God continued to provide food to Elijah, the woman, and her son.

Do you think you would have trusted Elijah as this woman did? If a stranger showed up at your door asking for money or food would you give it to them? While I would like to think that I would as a loving Christian, I cannot say for sure how I would react. In today's age we have been conditioned to question the legitimacy of others' needs, and this may or may not be rightfully so. We all too often hear stories of con artists who steal from people who just want to help. We fear that if we give a handout to someone, they will come back asking for more.

Now take this person requesting help one step further. Imagine that you are broke. Your house has been foreclosed, your farm is owned by the bank, your cupboards are nearly empty, and you are at the end of your road financially. You are out of options. Then a person shows up at your door saying they are in need of some food. Do you invite them in?

The widow showed great love to Elijah. She set the example of being a servant and trusting in God to provide. As a result, she did not eat her last meal that day. God continued to provide. God had allowed her to be in a situation of dire need. Yet he used her situation to teach people for thousands of years about the need to trust in him. I doubt this story would have the same effect on us if Elijah had showed up at the doors of a wealthy man who still had five years of food in stock.

No matter what type of troubles we face, God is with us. We may feel alone or wonder why God allows us to face trouble, but he works through our troubles for good. Sometimes our troubles improve us, while at other times they are for the benefit of those around us. When God gives you a sticky situation, remember that he has a plan for you. And most important, he will be by your side for all of it.

Trust in the Dark

1 Kings 17:17–24

[17]Some time later the son of the woman who owned the house became ill. He grew worse and worse, and finally stopped breathing. [18]She said to Elijah, "What do you have against me, man of God? Did you come to remind me of my sin and kill my son?"

[19]"Give me your son," Elijah replied. He took him from her arms, carried him to the upper room where he was staying, and laid him on his bed. [20]Then he cried out to the LORD, "LORD my God, have you brought tragedy even on this widow I am staying with, by causing her son to die?" [21]Then he stretched himself out on the boy three times and cried out to the LORD, "LORD my God, let this boy's life return to him!"

[22]The LORD heard Elijah's cry, and the boy's life returned to him, and he lived. [23]Elijah picked up the child and carried him down from the room into the house. He gave him to his mother and said, "Look, your son is alive!"

[24]Then the woman said to Elijah, "Now I know that you are a man of God and that the word of the LORD from your mouth is the truth."

WHY DO BAD THINGS have to happen to good people? If I am a Christian, why doesn't God take better care of me? If God is love, why does he allow me to be in such suffering and pain?

As farmers, we can often question why God allows pain and suffering to fall upon us. It can feel frustrating to have pain if we honor him by going to church, praying regularly, giving him our extra time and money, and living our life as close to his laws as we possibly can. Why doesn't he reward us with a bountiful harvest? Why must we deal with the torments of the weather, toil so hard at our work, and get paid an amount that does not seem to compensate us for our work?

In the previous verses about Elijah and the widow, we saw that because of her generosity and faith that God would provide food, she was blessed with a continuing supply of food. Every day she would feel as if she were using the last of her flour, and there would always be more the next day. She shared her little wealth with others, and God continued to bless her.

Then her son became sick and died. She could not understand why this was happening to her. She had done God's will, yet her son died. She questioned God, and she questioned Elijah. She did not understand why she must suffer by seeing her son pass away before her.

As Elijah took the body of the boy, he prayed to God and asked the same question. Even the prophet Elijah could not understand why God had allowed this. He prayed and asked God to bring the boy back to life. God heard his prayer, and the boy was raised from the dead.

These verses do not tell us why God allowed the son to die, just as we often do not understand why pain happens in our life. Sometimes we get healing, and the pain goes away through joy. A sick person may return to health, and everyone can rejoice. Other times, the actions are not reversed. Death can take loved ones away, crops may be destroyed, or a fire may take a barn from us forever. The only healing for these situations may be the healing of time and moving on. We will come to accept the loss of a loved one, a new growing season will come, and a new barn will be built to replace the old.

In the end, God will continue to bless us and use whatever situations we experience to help us grow. For the widow, her faith increased greatly after her son was raised from the dead. God may choose other ways today to increase our faith. It may be learning to depend on him during tough times, or it may be asking for understanding and acceptance when strife hits our life. Whatever it may be, God knows our needs and will continue to provide.

One Hot Fire

1 Kings 18:36–38

³⁶At the time of sacrifice, the prophet Elijah stepped forward and prayed: "Lord, the God of Abraham, Isaac and Israel, let it be known today that you are God in Israel and that I am your servant and have done all these things at your command. ³⁷Answer me, Lord, answer me, so these people will know that you, Lord, are God, and that you are turning their hearts back again."

³⁸Then the fire of the Lord fell and burned up the sacrifice, the wood, the stones and the soil, and also licked up the water in the trench.

For the entire story of Elijah on Mount Carmel, read 1 Kings 18.

I enjoy making fires. It seems as if we are always burning something on the farm. We burn ditches and fence lines in the spring, we burn cardboard and old wood when we clean out buildings, and after a tree dies we burn up the brush. However, a fire only burns when the fuel is dry, and no matter how hot a fire is it seems like there are always leftovers for the next fire to clean up. There are some things that will not burn, such as metal or rocks that are mixed in with the flammable material.

Many of us are familiar with the story of Elijah on Mount Carmel in 1 Kings 18. Elijah has finally returned in the middle of the drought to visit King Ahab. It is time to face the followers of the false gods of Baal. Elijah challenges the 450 prophets of Baal to a type of showdown, in which each will offer sacrifices and ask their god to burn it. The followers of Baal are confident in their gods, so they gladly accept the challenge.

I cannot imagine being in Elijah's shoes. He was facing 450 prophets plus many other onlookers, such as the king, who were sure Baal was going to win. Elijah, however, was all alone. Can you imagine the fear of what would happen if these people turned on him? Yet Elijah did not waver in his faith. In fact, after the Baal worshipers failed to get their fire started, Elijah upped the ante.

Elijah first dug a trench around God's altar. He then had so much water dumped on it that it completely filled the trench around the altar. God had instructed Elijah that He would demonstrate His power that day. Elijah had to trust that God would deliver on this promise, and his faith allowed him to take these great measures. He was taking a significant risk. Yet Elijah knew it was not *his* power but God's. He said a prayer and stepped back.

When God's fire burned, it burned with a terrifying fury. It consumed not only the sacrifice, but also the stones, soil, and all the water. I have made some hot fires in my time, but I have never burned rock. In fact, I have never seen a fire just explode out of nowhere. I always need to light it. God left no room for questions or what-ifs. It was clear to all the people standing on that mountain who the real God was.

When we read stories from the Bible that demonstrate signs of power from God, it can make us wish sometimes that God would do something like that today. While I would be hesitant if a pastor stepped forward and told people that he could call fire down from heaven, God does give us signs of his power today. The beauty of nature is seen daily in the sunrise, in the fact that a crop can be produced from a tiny seed, or that God can grow human and animal life through a cycle of baby to adult. Despite the many accomplishments of human beings, we have not even come close to the miracles God puts in nature. We also see God's miracles when humans are rescued from disaster, sick people make recoveries that go beyond the explanation of medicine, and people show compassion even in the darkest hours.

God is still performing miracles today. The question is, are you willing to recognize them? Do you accept them as miracles of God, or do you write them off as science with no influence from God? Sometimes he slaps us in the face with expressions of his power, but we need to open our eyes to see them. When the night falls, do not forget to thank God for his wonderful gifts.

Remembering God on Good Days

1 Kings 18:39–45

³⁹When all the people saw this, they fell prostrate and cried, "The LORD—he is God! The LORD—he is God!"

⁴⁰Then Elijah commanded them, "Seize the prophets of Baal. Don't let anyone get away!" They seized them, and Elijah had them brought down to the Kishon Valley and slaughtered there.

⁴¹And Elijah said to Ahab, "Go, eat and drink, for there is the sound of a heavy rain." ⁴²So Ahab went off to eat and drink, but Elijah climbed to the top of Carmel, bent down to the ground and put his face between his knees.

⁴³"Go and look toward the sea," he told his servant. And he went up and looked.

"There is nothing there," he said.

Seven times Elijah said, "Go back."

⁴⁴The seventh time the servant reported, "A cloud as small as a man's hand is rising from the sea."

So Elijah said, "Go and tell Ahab, 'Hitch up your chariot and go down before the rain stops you.'"

⁴⁵Meanwhile, the sky grew black with clouds, the wind rose, a heavy rain started falling and Ahab rode off to Jezreel.

I CAN REMEMBER numerous times in my life when a thunderstorm has rolled through, ending a long drought. It is always amazing how good the pouring rain feels. The smell of the rain on the ground is nostalgic. After many days of working in dusty conditions or feeling worn out from irrigating to keep the crops alive, the rain truly feels like a gift from God.

Imagine being the people of Israel. They had not received any rain for a few years. Famine was probably setting in as food supplies dried up and water sources were becoming scarce, and the dust must have been awful. God told Elijah that the rain was going to come again, so Elijah sent his servant to go watch the sky. Six times the servant returned with nothing to report. The seventh time, the servant noticed a small cloud forming. Whether they were farmers or not, surely all the people were affected by the drought. Rain was a blessing to everyone in the land.

God had brought the drought on the land to turn the people back to him and away from the false gods of Baal. But after years of drought they still believed in Baal. Then God showed his power twice in one day. First, he burned Elijah's sacrifice. This caused the people to turn on the prophets of Baal and kill them. Now God was returning rain to the land. It would take time to win everybody over, but more people began to return their trust to the true God.

God blesses us each time it rains. It sometimes feels ironic how drought is often followed by lots of rain. I can think of a number of times when, less than a week after a drought ends, we experience flooding. I like to think that God wants to keep reminding us that he is in control. I must admit that, while I remember to ask God for rain during the drought, a prayer of thanks is often forgotten or only said in passing when the rain comes. Certainly God wants to be there to listen to our struggles, but he also wants to be with us on every ordinary day. If you only talk to a friend when you experience troubles, your friendship is going to lack the substance needed to keep it a friendship. God also wants to be more than just a counselor. He wants to be with us each and every day. While I do not think every bad thing in our lives happens because we stray from God, I also figure we should not force God to send struggles just so we will remember him. Keep God in your heart each and every day.

Pressing On

Philippians 3:12–14

[12]Not that I have already obtained all this, or have already arrived at my goal, but I press on to take hold of that for which Christ Jesus took hold of me. [13]Brothers and sisters, I do not consider myself yet to have taken hold of it. But one thing I do: Forgetting what is behind and straining toward what is ahead, [14]I press on toward the goal to win the prize for which God has called me heavenward in Christ Jesus.

THERE COMES A POINT in our strawberry season when things begin to wind down. We have picked strawberries for three solid weeks, and it feels as if it has been three months. Those three weeks may be the most demanding of the year. There is a sense of relief, as we know there are only a few days left. The customers begin to thin out, we pick a little less each day, and the picking becomes easier and easier. At this point, it would be easy to just coast and go through the motions until the season is over.

However, coasting would not be the best choice. As much as we might be ready for a few days off, we are still open and our customers are still coming. When they drive onto our farm, they do not care that our season is almost over. They came to get strawberries, and they expect the same treatment they received for the past three weeks. Meanwhile, we know that our next season of summer produce is just around the corner. There will be lots of preparation for the next season. Our other crops are still growing, and there is plenty of hoeing, tilling, and spraying that needs to be done. Until the snow flies, our season is not over.

As Christians, we also have times when we are ready to coast. We feel like we have been so involved with church and immersed so deeply in God's word that it may be time for a little break. Why not take it easy for a little while? We know that we are strong in our faith, and a little time off may help us. To some degree, our involvement in our church or community may indeed need this break. Even pastors will take a sabbatical from time to time in order to focus. However, our relationship with God should not take sabbaticals.

Paul says, "I do not consider myself to have taken hold of it." Christianity is not about putting in your time until you have earned heaven. Heaven is a gift, and God expects us to have a relationship with him for our whole lives. Even if we feel like we have done great things, the future always holds potential. We need to forget our past, whether it is glamorous or ugly, and continue to push toward a stronger relationship with Christ. Until our day of heaven comes, we should always be pushing toward God.

Feeding the Ark

Genesis 6:19–22

[19]"You are to bring into the ark two of all living creatures, male and female, to keep them alive with you. [20]Two of every kind of bird, of every kind of animal and of every kind of creature that moves along the ground will come to you to be kept alive. [21]You are to take every kind of food that is to be eaten and store it away as food for you and for them."

[22]Noah did everything just as God commanded him.

I HAD THE OPPORTUNITY one year to work at a food bank, handing out special Thanksgiving dinners. At the beginning of the day, we had a mountain of food to distribute. In a few short hours, around five hundred families passed through our line and received food for their dinners. Our mountain of food quickly disappeared. The thing that struck me was how much food was distributed to serve just one meal. When I looked at this stockpile it was depressing to consider how much food it would take to feed all those who are needy and hungry all over the world every day.

Noah must have felt a similar fear as he received his instructions from God to build the ark. When God told him to go build an ark of epic proportions, he was probably stunned at the amount of work it would take. I am willing to guess it took him a day or two before realized that he would also need to feed all those animals that he was supposed to bring along.

Noah was on the ark for over a year. Imagine the work in Old Testament times, using mainly hand tools, to raise the food for even one family for a single year. But Noah had to produce enough food for at least two of every animal. He then had to store it in a giant boat, which was also on his to-do list. While we do not know exactly how long he had to prepare, we can estimate from context that Noah spent around fifty to a hundred years preparing for the flood.

For a man who was six hundred years old when the flood came, this period of time was probably not overly significant in terms of his entire lifespan. Yet time did not pass any faster in the Old Testament. Imagine spending that many years building an ark and filling it with food for a flood that is yet to come, to feed a bunch of animals you may have never seen! I would certainly not have had the faith of Noah.

God still asks us to live our lives on faith. Do you trust God to lead your daily decisions? Are you following God's call for your life? God does have a plan for each of us. Some plans involve much of our lives, such as our families and our careers. Other plans may occur on a daily basis, such as how we impact those we encounter. God probably will not ask you to do anything so great as to build an ark to save the world, but how will you answer his smaller calls?

Stubborn

Matthew 11:20–24

[20]Then Jesus began to denounce the towns in which most of his miracles had been performed, because they did not repent. [21]"Woe to you, Chorazin! Woe to you, Bethsaida! For if the miracles that were performed in you had been performed in Tyre and Sidon, they would have repented long ago in sack-cloth and ashes. [22]But I tell you, it will be more bearable for Tyre and Sidon on the day of judgment than for you. [23]And you, Capernaum, will you be lifted to the heavens? No, you will go down to Hades. For if the miracles that were performed in you had been performed in Sodom, it would have re-mained to this day. [24]But I tell you that it will be more bearable for Sodom on the day of judgment than for you."

ARE YOU KNOWN to be stubborn? Do you refuse to do something even though you know you should? I think farmers often make choices that they know could be dangerous. Sometimes, as we are fixing an electric fence, we know it should be turned off. But walking around to turn it off would take too much effort, so we keep tinkering, hoping we do not get shocked. We know that riding on the hitch of a tractor may not be the safest thing, but it was a long day and we don't want to walk. Or you may tell yourself that it will take too long to shut off the auger, and it will clean out better if you leave it run. So you risk injury as you work too close to it.

Most of us have probably been guilty of one of these situations at some point in time, and I am sure you can think of many others. We know that all of these situations are dangerous, but for some reason we think that the hurt and pain will not apply to us. We are smarter than that, we think, and would not let ourselves get hurt. Unfortunately, thousands of people with this men-tality get hurt each year.

Jesus was dealing with some very stubborn people too. He had been traveling for some time teaching, preaching, and performing great miracles. Some people were amazed at what he had done, and crowds came to listen to him. However, Jesus was also able to look into their hearts. He knew that, though they were listening, the message was not sinking into their hearts. They heard the words and knew what they needed to do, but decided it would be better to simply ignore Jesus' teachings. They were not moved by what he was doing.

How stubborn are you? How do you answer God when he calls? Sometimes we are so busy trying to figure out what we should do in our lives that we miss God's finger pointing where we should go. We may even pray for guidance, but are only asking God to give us the answer that *we* want. We are not listening for the answer that *he* wants to give.

Our stubbornness can prevent us from doing God's will. What can we do to change this? Prayer is certainly an important step. Even though God knows our thoughts and needs, the action of praying lets our minds release our struggles to God. This helps open a doorway in our minds. Being immersed in God's word is also important. I have been amazed by how God has used devotion topics, Bible study verses, and even readings or sermons in church to address my current concerns. I did not seek this out, but by being involved with those activities he found a way to talk to me.

Finally, continue to be surrounded by Christians who will build up your faith. God certainly works through others, and he may put what you need to hear into someone else's mouth. Be open with others and find a core group of people who can help you build your faith.

It can be easy to be stubborn. As you go about your life, try to put your stubbornness aside. Let God's will be done in your spiritual life, and stay safe in your farm life.

Selective Breeding

Genesis 30:37–43

[37]Jacob, however, took fresh-cut branches from poplar, almond and plane trees and made white stripes on them by peeling the bark and exposing the white inner wood of the branches. [38]Then he placed the peeled branches in all the watering troughs, so that they would be directly in front of the flocks when they came to drink. When the flocks were in heat and came to drink, [39]they mated in front of the branches. And they bore young that were streaked or speckled or spotted. [40]Jacob set apart the young of the flock by themselves, but made the rest face the streaked and dark-colored animals that belonged to Laban. Thus he made separate flocks for himself and did not put them with Laban's animals. [41]Whenever the stronger females were in heat, Jacob would place the branches in the troughs in front of the animals so they would mate near the branches, [42]but if the animals were weak, he would not place them there. So the weak animals went to Laban and the strong ones to Jacob. [43]In this way the man grew exceedingly prosperous and came to own large flocks, and maidservants and menservants, and camels and donkeys.

For the entire story of Jacob breeding Laban's flocks, read Genesis 30 and 31.

WHEN I READ THROUGH GENESIS 30, I was a little surprised because this was a story I was not familiar with. For some reason, Jacob's plot to steal Laban's flocks through selective breeding is not part of a typical Sunday reading. Yet it is one of the longest stories about farming in the Bible, so let's take a look at it.

Remember that Jacob had fled to his uncle Laban because his brother Esau was mad that Jacob had stolen his birthright. Jacob fell in love with Laban's youngest daughter Rachel, and Laban agreed to let Jacob marry her if he worked for seven years. However, Laban tricked him into marrying his older daughter Leah. So Jacob had to work seven more years to marry Rachel.

After fourteen-plus years of dedicated service, Laban was willing to share part of his wealth and give Jacob a few sheep in exchange to keep Jacob working for him.

Jacob worked out a deal with Laban. Jacob would take all the spotted and discolored sheep, while Laban would keep all the nicely colored animals. But Jacob had a plan. He would place colored sticks near the flock's water. Because of this, the spotted sheep would breed with the un-patterned sheep. Since Jacob was entitled to any speckled sheep, his flocks quickly grew, because the newborn animals were mostly spotted. After just a few years, he now owned most of Laban's flock through his selective breeding program.

The thing that struck me about this story when I first read it was the trickery Jacob used. However, as we see in the surrounding chapters, this is not the first time Jacob used his wits to acquire things that were not his. He even stole his brother's birthright by tricking his father into thinking he was Esau.

Remember that Laban was not very honest with Jacob either. He made promises that he broke. He did not want Jacob to leave, but God had other plans. Jacob's family would someday be the twelve tribes of Israel. In later verses we learn that God gave Jacob this plan. He had a plan to deliver Jacob from Laban. A few hundred years later God would give Moses a plan to deliver Israel from Egypt. Many more years later God fulfilled his plan to deliver all humans from sin, and a baby was born in a manger. Do you think that stable had any speckled sheep?

God still has a plan for every one of us. Whether it is a plan for our lives here on earth, or his final plan of eternal life in heaven for all believers, God has a plan. We may not know all the steps of the process, but we have read the last chapter. Jesus has told us that he is going to heaven to prepare a place for us. That is a plan worth waiting for.

The Wolf and the Lamb

Isaiah 11:6–10

⁶The wolf will live with the lamb,
 the leopard will lie down with the goat,
the calf and the lion and the yearling together;
 and a little child will lead them.
⁷The cow will feed with the bear,
 their young will lie down together,
 and the lion will eat straw like the ox.
⁸The infant will play near the cobra's den,
 the young child will put its hand into the viper's nest.
⁹They will neither harm nor destroy
 on all my holy mountain,
for the earth will be filled with the knowledge of the LORD
 as the waters cover the sea.
¹⁰In that day the Root of Jesse will stand as a banner for the peoples; the nations will rally to him, and his resting place will be glorious.

I HAVE NEVER HEARD of farmers having too many problems with lions and leopards in my home state of Wisconsin. Those beasts are not very common here! However, wolves tend to be a problem for farmers in northern Wisconsin. Wolves are interesting—they are not that large, but when they work in packs they can be deadly. Farmers struggle to keep the wolves away from their livestock, but there is little they can do. Wolves are considered endangered, even though they are overpopulated in areas of Wisconsin. When the wolves get too crowded and too hungry, they make raids on local farms.

Wolves are not usually thought of as calm, loving animals. They are beasts of prey. Leopards, lions, and cobras are also not perceived of as the most gentle of animals. However, Isaiah prophesies about a day when these animals will coexist with the lamb, goat, calf, cow, and children. Why would these animals come together if they knew they could be killed?

God promises repeatedly in the Bible that one day he will take the believers to heaven. There will be peace and security there. In heaven we will not worry about who will cause us harm or who may be waiting to stab us in the back. In heaven we will not worry about who is Catholic, Lutheran, Methodist, Baptist, or any other Christian denomination. We will not worry about what specific type of liquid Jesus specified to be his blood for communion or when is the best time to sing hymns during church.

God will celebrate the millions of people who have loved him. God will look at our hearts. He will look to see if we believe that Jesus is our savior and that our only way to heaven is through our humble acceptance of a gift that we did not earn. God expects us to live our lives for him here on earth. The many Christian denominations of this world can be confusing to Christians. Within our groups we may choose to follow God and his commands in slightly different ways. But as we test the claims of different groups, we can look at Jesus' gift as a promise that we will one day be in heaven together.

Until then, we continue to study God's word and become stronger in each of our faiths. We also have the opportunity to support those of other denominations. While we may feel like the wolf and the lamb sometimes, if we take more time to get to know each other and work together we may grow in ways we never expected. In the end, we are striving to complete God's work.

Modern Miracles

Psalm 104:1, 10–14

¹Praise the LORD, my soul.

LORD my God, you are very great;

you are clothed with splendor and majesty.

¹⁰He makes springs pour water into the ravines;

it flows between the mountains.

¹¹They give water to all the beasts of the field;

the wild donkeys quench their thirst.

¹²The birds of the sky nest by the waters;

they sing among the branches.

¹³He waters the mountains from his upper chambers;

the land is satisfied by the fruit of his work.

¹⁴He makes grass grow for the cattle,

and plants for people to cultivate—

bringing forth food from the earth.

PLANTING A CORNFIELD can be a humbling experience. Wait . . . you have never felt humbled by planting a cornfield? If not, consider this: First, you dump into your planter bags of seed that weigh around 50 pounds. Each 50-pound bag probably holds about 80,000 seeds, which should be enough to plant around three to four acres. Taking the conservative approach of three acres, that seed could produce around 180 bushels per acre, or about 540 bushels of corn. Assuming a 15.5 percent moisture content, making the corn weigh 56 pounds per bushel, this corn would weigh 30,240 pounds. We started with just 50 pounds of seed and ended up with 30,240 pounds of corn.

Still not amazed? Consider what happens after you dump in the seed. With a loaded planter you begin driving across the field at about five miles per hour. Either a plate or vacuum is putting seeds in the ground at break-neck speeds. At five miles an hour you are traveling 7.3 feet per second, so with an 8-inch spacing you plant almost 11 seeds per second per row. If you have ever listened to a city person talk about gardening, you know that growing a plant is not always successful, as some people can never seem to get their seeds to even sprout out of the ground. Yet you can plant a seed every tenth of a second (times the number of rows you plant!), and most will grow and be successful.

Certainly your success as a farmer will depend on how you use and calibrate your tractors, GPS, fertilizer, pest management, and a wide array of other resources. We know there is a lot more to farming than just putting a seed into the ground. Yet God's hand is certainly at work in his harvest. We could plant a bag of pea gravel and give it all the nutrients we want, but it is not going to produce anything. God has not given gravel the ability to reproduce.

As we look back at miracles in the Bible, such as God feeding the five thousand with only a few loaves of bread and fish, it seems like an unrealistic fairytale. Even with knowledge that Jesus produced amazing miracles while he was here in the flesh, it can seem like God has forgotten to produce any miracles for a long time.

To get 30,240 pounds of food out of a 50-pound bag seems quite amazing to me. As humans we may be able to manufacture incredible things, but it always takes more raw input than what we get in output. God, however, is able to produce more from less. Whether they are the "springs that pour water into the ravines" or the fact that "He makes grass grow for the cattle," God performs amazing miracles for us. He provides us with food and everything else we need.

As farmers, God has tasked us with caring for his resources. Take this trust with pride and do your best in the work that you do. When the harvest comes and it is good, remember to thank God for it.

Common Understanding

Hebrews 4:14–16

[14]Therefore, since we have a great high priest who has ascended into heaven, Jesus the Son of God, let us hold firmly to the faith we profess. [15]For we do not have a high priest who is unable to empathize with our weaknesses, but we have one who has been tempted in every way, just as we are—yet he did not sin. [16]Let us then approach God's throne of grace with confidence, so that we may receive mercy and find grace to help us in our time of need.

I LIVE IN A COMMUNITY that would not really be considered an agricultural community. While the cities in our county are surrounded by farms, a population of over 125,000 does not make our area very rural. Needless to say, the majority of the people I come in contact with are not farmers. They do not have any idea what farmers really do for a living.

Maybe you have experienced some of the interesting questions or simply stupid comments from others. I feel that people do not understand that we really do work seven days a week, and that farmers work more than an eight-hour day. It can annoy me when someone from town gets out of their car at my house and exclaims, "Oh my, welcome to the country! It stinks here!" My favorite comment, or should I say *least* favorite comment, is along the lines of: "It must be nice to only have to work five months a year."

I am willing to guess you have experienced some of these situations before, and you can probably think of other examples. Most of the time we can write off comments like these as naive and choose to ignore them. The truth is, we probably do not understand the other person's job very well either. Yet when we are having a bad day, are under lots of pressure, or are a little too tired, comments like these can rub us the wrong way.

Hopefully there are people in your life who do understand your job, family, and way of life. Whether they are family members, neighbors, or fellow farmers in a farm organization, there is comfort in being in the company of those who understand. These people are sharing in our daily battle. When we do something, there is peace in knowing that someone else is going through the same type of struggles, because we feel a sense of their resilience too.

As Christians, we also face struggles, but we are lucky to have a strong network of fellow Christians to help support us in what we do each day. Hebrews 4 talks about another person who can relate to us: Jesus. God is God, and he could have chosen any way to save the world that he wanted. Yet he chose to send his son Jesus to live on earth for more than thirty years. As a man, Jesus experienced our struggles exactly as we do.

Jesus was tempted by sin. Jesus grew hungry, tired, and overwhelmed. Jesus suffered pain and betrayal. He experienced human life. Yet, through all these challenges, he faced the pressure to save the world. He lived a blameless life without sin, and we can now receive a promise of heaven because of him. We can tell him our problems, and he will understand our struggles because he has been in our shoes. Let this be a comfort, knowing that you do not walk alone.

Child's Work

1 Samuel 17:33–37

[33]Saul replied, "You are not able to go out against this Philistine and fight him; you are only a boy, and he has been a fighting man from his youth."

[34]But David said to Saul, "Your servant has been keeping his father's sheep. When a lion or a bear came and carried off a sheep from the flock, [35]I went after it, struck it and rescued the sheep from its mouth. When it turned on me, I seized it by its hair, struck it and killed it. [36]Your servant has killed both the lion and the bear; this uncircumcised Philistine will be like one of them, because he has defied the armies of the living God. [37]The LORD who delivered me from the paw of the lion and the paw of the bear will deliver me from the hand of this Philistine."

Saul said to David, "Go, and the LORD be with you."

DO YOU REMEMBER what it was like when you first began doing farm chores? How old were you? Were you given lots of training, or were you given a quick explanation and then sent off to work on your own? Since the beginning of time, children and teenagers have played an important part on the family farm. Children in biblical times helped to tend flocks and care for the animals. I remember reading books as a child, such as the *Little House on the Prairie* series and *Caddie Woodlawn*, in which the children were important in helping their fathers and mothers care for the farm. Today, the government debates the safety concerns of children on the farm.

No matter what time period you look at, children are still children on the farm. In some cases, they are given full responsibility at a very young age because their parents know they can handle it and are willing to pass some work to them. Other times, there are thirty-year-old children who are not given the opportunity to make any decisions for the farm. It is interesting to see how so many families and situations can be so different. In my experience, though, the trust usually comes from the parents.

Outsiders look at children and wonder if they can really handle any adult tasks. They do not know what the child has learned and done; nor do they know the child's potential. They may even compare the skills of a seventeen-year-old to those of a ten-year-old and not recognize the difference in maturity and skills because both are considered children. Sometimes young farmers are inhibited by their size and age rather than by their skills.

David faced this struggle too. No man was brave enough to fight Goliath, but David knew he had been preparing a long time for this. He also knew that God was with him. King Saul looked at David and only saw a boy. He did not recognize the unique skills David had acquired as a shepherd. David may not have been trained to use the spears and swords of the army, but he had killed both lions and bears while protecting his father's flocks. He trusted that God had protected him and had given him power over those beasts, and he trusted that God would protect him again.

David had spent his short life using his skills to prepare for the future. If you have children, you may wonder what their future will bring. Will they choose to farm too? What happens if they choose to find work away from the farm, or even away from agriculture? While you may want them to choose their own path, it can still be hard for some to see them leave the farm. However, God has used their time spent on the farm to build their skills, knowledge, and work ethic, and those will be an important part of their future. When Jacob sent David to care for his flocks, he probably did not guess that David would one day kill a giant to save the land. He probably did not guess that David would eventually leave the farm to become king. You may not know what God has in store for your children, and they may not either. Yet we do know that God has a plan for each of us, and he uses our whole life to achieve that plan. Trust God's plan, wherever it may lead.

Forgive and Forget

Matthew 18:23–35 (NKJV)

[23]Therefore the kingdom of heaven is like a certain king who wanted to settle accounts with his servants. [24]And when he had begun to settle accounts, one was brought to him who owed him ten thousand talents. [25]But as he was not able to pay, his master commanded that he be sold, with his wife and children and all that he had, and that payment be made. [26]The servant therefore fell down before him, saying, 'Master, have patience with me, and I will pay you all.' [27]Then the master of that servant was moved with compassion, released him, and forgave him the debt.

[28]"But that servant went out and found one of his fellow servants who owed him a hundred denarii; and he laid hands on him and took him by the throat, saying, 'Pay me what you owe!' [29]So his fellow servant fell down at his feet and begged him, saying, 'Have patience with me, and I will pay you all.' [30]And he would not, but went and threw him into prison till he should pay the debt. [31]So when his fellow servants saw what had been done, they were very grieved, and came and told their master all that had been done. [32]Then his master, after he had called him, said to him, 'You wicked servant! I forgave you all that debt because you begged me. [33]Should you not also have had compassion on your fellow servant, just as I had pity on you?' [34]And his master was angry, and delivered him to the torturers until he should pay all that was due to him.

[35]"So My heavenly Father also will do to you if each of you, from his heart, does not forgive his brother his trespasses."

HAVE YOU BEEN holding a grudge? Is there someone who really irritates you? In rural neighborhoods, grudges can be all too common. Neighbors can get along great for years, but one event can suddenly change everything. People can go from being friends to not talking to each other at all. The grudge can quickly spread through the neighborhood. Dividing lines are drawn, and two camps form. This process can occur gradually, without anyone realizing the magnitude of the situation.

The danger with standing grudges is that sometimes we do not even know why we do not like the other party. The grudge may even have been handed down from a previous generation, and we do not get along with others simply because that is the way it has always been. We may find small imperfections in others, but in our minds those minor characteristics make that person evil. We simply cannot imagine talking to, sharing with, or being a friend to that person.

Grudges can be dangerous because they weaken our love for others. In the parable of the unmerciful servant, Jesus talks about the most important reason we should forgive others. Despite all our flaws and mistakes, God still loves us and forgives us when we ask. Our flaws are great, yet he forgives us. We must humble ourselves, but he still loves us.

His love is great, but if we are choosing not to give forgiveness to others, we show God that we are ungrateful for the gift he has given us. Forgiveness given to others is a gift to God for his gift to us. Sometimes it is hard for us to be forgiving and try to maintain a friendly relationship with others. The other person may even not want to return your forgiveness and friendliness, and may continue to dislike you. However, if you don't humble yourself your relationship may never go anywhere.

Make a commitment today to put some past disagreements behind you. Make an effort to visit a friend or neighbor whom you have not seen eye to eye with for a while, and try to extend a hand of love. God asks us to love even our enemies, but sometimes our enemies can turn out to be our friends.

Born in a Barn

Luke 2:4–7

⁴So Joseph also went up from the town of Nazareth in Galilee to Judea, to Bethlehem the town of David, because he belonged to the house and line of David. ⁵He went there to register with Mary, who was pledged to be married to him and was expecting a child. ⁶While they were there, the time came for the baby to be born, ⁷and she gave birth to her firstborn, a son. She wrapped him in cloths and placed him in a manger, because there was no guest room available for them.

"WERE YOU BORN IN A BARN?" I have never really understood the origins of the phrase, but it is often used when someone forgets to close a door or makes a mess. Apparently if you are born in a barn you have no manners. I have met people who were born at home rather than in a hospital, but I have never met someone who was actually born in a barn, as our savior was.

God has a plan for our lives, but we do not always understand what his plan may be. I can imagine Mary was wondering what God was thinking when she was told she would have to have her baby in a barn. God had already told her to trust him with this baby issue that had come up, and she knew he would make things work according to his will. Yet she had to be wondering what was going on as they wandered from inn to inn, looking without success for a place to stay. Why hadn't God called in a reservation?

Throughout his ministry, Jesus spent time associating with those who were considered lower-class. Note that shepherds visited him first, not kings. He was not coming to be power and might, and he could be most recognized by those who were willing to accept him as Lord.

Jesus came into a messy world full of sin and evil. His job would be to save it. He was born in a barn that was probably full of filth, manure, dirt, and foul odors. It was not exactly a normal maternity ward. God could have sat by in heaven and researched other ways to save his people. However, he chose to come to earth, immerse himself in the sin-stained world, and lead the world to light.

If you leave a door open, people may say that you were born in a barn. God opened a door that first Christmas. He opened a door to heaven. He came to earth through the door, and when he rose into heaven he passed back through the door. Jesus never closed the door, though. In fact, it is still wide open today. Open doors encourage us to come inside, and Jesus invites us to come through his door. He is the doorway to heaven.

When we put our faith in Jesus and trust that he is the door, we have the promise of heaven. In John 14:6 Jesus says, "No one comes to the Father except through me." We cannot earn heaven, or find the way on our own. We must live our life following Jesus. When we get to the end of our road, he will carry us home. I am proud to say my savior was born in a barn.

Thankful for the Little Things

1 Thessalonians 5:16–18
[16]Rejoice always, [17]pray continually, [18]give thanks in all circumstances; for this is God's will for you in Christ Jesus.

I HAVE HAD DAYS on the farm that have been less than ideal. Trying the fourth replacement part on the tractor and discovering it is still not the right one. Meanwhile, other problems are growing while I keep trying to fix this one. I also have days that go quite well. Nothing breaks, no one gets hurt, and I accomplish a satisfying amount of work. At the end of both of these days, I go home at night and my day is over. I may be in a slightly better mood in one case, but I rarely go home from work on the farm with a fresh skip in my step and a song in my mouth, ready to conquer the world. Usually I am just tired after a long day.

There is a real danger in becoming complacent in our normal surroundings. Think of someone who lives on the edge of a mountain range. The mountains are a normal view and the person may not think much about them. Yet someone who visits from outside the area may be amazed at the beauty. People who visit our farm are often amazed by how far they can see. I am never that impressed with our view of a few miles, and the hills and woods in the distance. But to someone who normally stares out their back window at a house fifty feet away, my view is amazing.

The fact is, we are surrounded with beauty and other things to be grateful for. I admit that I can be a victim of only looking to God when times are tough. When the going is good, God gets forgotten much more easily. As I walk home I do not even think about how much God blessed me with a good day when nothing broke. I forget that he kept me safe, provides me with work, and makes my farm productive. It is not that I do not recognize that all these gifts come from God; just that I become complacent with the gifts that he gives me. I allow other things to fill my mind, and I do not leave room to talk with God.

Paul gives the Thessalonians three commands in three short verses. First, we need to rejoice always. Make a conscious effort each day to be happy and thankful for the little things. If you think something is too insignificant to be thankful for, wait until it breaks or causes problems. I have numerous muscles that I never even know exist until I do something to hurt one of them. I should be thankful that they simply do their job ninety-nine percent of the time without me knowing it. Make an effort to thank God throughout your day.

As we continually rejoice, we can follow Paul's second piece of advice: to pray continually. Many times we limit our prayers to prayers of need. We may sneak a thank you in here or there, but we come to God most often with needs. Asking God for help is not wrong. He wants to be involved in all our struggles. Yet God also wants to celebrate the good. Offer prayers of thanks throughout your day. A three-second prayer is fine. If you can say twenty short thank-you prayers during your day, your relationship with God will grow. When this becomes habit, you will find your conversations with God increasing each day.

Finally, Paul reminds us to always give thanks, no matter what the situation. Yes, we will have hard times. We may not be yelling out "Alleluia!" when times are tough, but we can still give thanks. Continue to give thanks to God for the small positive things in every day. Then you can come to God with a humble heart and ask for his help. Be involved with God continually in all that you say and do.

Is Farming a Sin?

Genesis 8:15–17

[15]Then God said to Noah, [16]"Come out of the ark, you and your wife and your sons and their wives. [17]Bring out every kind of living creature that is with you—the birds, the animals, and all the creatures that move along the ground—so they can multiply on the earth and be fruitful and increase in number on it."

IMAGINE WHAT IT WAS like to be Noah walking off the ark. As he looked down on the new land he was about to inhabit, there were no animals. No birds flew overhead, no animals came running by, and no insects buzzed in the distance. The land was desolate of all breathing life. Even after the animals were released from the ark, the land was not exactly overpopulated with animals. It was still mostly bare.

God has always been a farmer of sorts. He grows plants to replace dead vegetation, and he made sure that the animals would reproduce to fill the land. All the animals and livestock today are descendants of animals that walked off the ark. God still cares for his people and animals today, although some understand his method of caring differently than others.

Some animal rights groups today claim that farmers harm livestock by keeping them in captivity. Yet as farmers we care for our animals by providing them with food, water, and shelter. We care for them in sickness. God wanted all of his creatures, including humans, to reproduce and fill the earth. As farmers we not only care for animals; we also care for people by providing food.

Sometimes we may be questioned by extreme groups as to how we can keep animals in captivity and still be Christians. Maybe I am missing something, but I do not remember Jesus forbidding people to care for animals to benefit people. In fact, Jesus used farm animals on multiple occasions for his work. Think about Palm Sunday, when he rode into Jerusalem on a domesticated donkey. When Jesus drove a demon out of a man, he sent it into a herd of pigs. Jesus even went fishing with his disciples after his resurrection.

Certainly, God expects us to care for his animals, as we should carefully manage all of creation. He has tasked us farmers with providing good care for them. If we didn't do so, we would be harming God's blessings and creation and failing to do what he has entrusted us to do. We help his creation to continue to increase and fill the earth. While we may sometimes feel in control of this process because of scientific advances such as artificial insemination, it is still God's hand that grows and cares for that fetus until and after the time it is born. The miracles of growth and life still rest in God's hands. As we carry out his work, we can take pride in continuing to fulfill a command given thousands of years ago, when the rebirth of the world began.

Good in God's Sight

1 Chronicles 19:13

¹³Be strong, and let us fight bravely for our people and the cities of our God. The LORD will do what is good in his sight.

I HAD THE OPPORTUNITY to visit some farms in the country of Peru during a mission trip. I was in a mountainous region that had small plots of land— usually an acre or less per family—that relied on the river in the valley for all water, because they received less than an inch of rain each year. A large river flowed down the steep mountains and this allowed irrigation ditches to carry water to fields within a mile of the river. Above the irrigation ditches, though, there was no vegetation.

Life was not easy for the farmers living there, and they had faced a number of problems over the years. A few people were Christians, but it was hard with few Christian resources, and their last priest had left a few years earlier with the key to the church. Before that, the church in that area had been corrupt and harmful to the people. Then, on August 15, 2007, an earthquake measuring 8.0 on the Richter scale struck about a hundred miles away from the town I visited.

The town had received lots of damage to buildings and structures, and the earthquake also damaged some of the irrigation canals that were so vital to the farmers. There would be no way to survive without the water. Government and nongovernmental organizations came in to help. One person sent to the area was a young missionary from a Lutheran World Mission group. He was one of the first people from the organization to be placed in Peru for an extended period of time.

As he began to work there, opportunities became available for him to slowly begin working with some of the people who wanted to have God in their lives. It was not easy, and it would take a few years before God sent more missionaries to help him and give his work direction. Yet by the time I visited, a few years later, God was starting to make his plan a little more visible to those working there. Six months after I left, his plan continued to become more visible as the one-man team had grown to over ten missionaries working to build a church and share God's love in various areas of Peru.

This small agricultural town probably would not have been the first choice of a place to start a church. The capital, Lima, would seem to be a better choice, and later the group did relocate its headquarters there. Yet God knew these local people needed the hope of Christ. When the earthquake struck it had devastating effects, and life still may not have been as nice as it had been before the earthquake. Yet God had a plan, and he has given Christ to this region in a way they least expected it. God does what is good in his sight.

Each day we try to do the will of God, and this is pleasing to him. However, we do not always know what his will may be. We may feel like we are failing, but it may simply be that God has different plans at the moment. Yet when we fight for God and do his work, we can let him take control. We may not understand what he is doing, but he will make it good in his sight.

From a Tiny Seed

Luke 13:18–19

[18]Then Jesus asked, "What is the kingdom of God like? What shall I compare it to? [19]It is like a mustard seed, which a man took and planted in his garden. It grew and became a tree, and the birds perched in its branches."

JESUS CAME TO EARTH, but he was not always a popular person here. We think of the choirs of angels at his birth, but at the same time, King Herod was trying to find the baby and kill him. Throughout Jesus' ministry there were those who did not believe what he was teaching. Once, a crowd even tried to throw him off a cliff. Jesus had to avoid certain areas for periods of time to avoid being killed.

Crowds did follow Jesus, and some believed what he taught. These people were taking a risk listening to this rogue prophet who was teaching some things that went against the priests of the church. For the people of his time, his teachings seemed radical. Today we look back at Jesus as an obvious choice, but he was not all that glamorous to the people of his time.

Therefore, the early Christian church was not very large. The fear of the Jews among the few followers of Jesus after his death added more anxiety. People like Saul rounded up Christians to kill them. The Jewish church rejected Jesus, and growth was hard.

Yet Jesus had spoken in parable about the church. He talked about a mustard seed. A mustard seed is very small, about the size of a cotton seed. However, it eventually grows up to be a large tree. This growth does not happen overnight. It needs sun, water, nutrients, and tending. It is only through work that a tree can grow. As farmers, we know the miracle of how something large and great can come from a tiny seed. Think of an entire field of crops that you can grow from a few bags of seed.

Jesus knew his church would not consume the world overnight. It started with just a small group of people, but it would grow. God sent the Holy Spirit on Pentecost to be with the apostles and help them grow the church. Through the Spirit the apostles added thousands of new believers at one time. God's church slowly began to grow.

God's church continues to grow today. Just like the mustard tree branches out far and wide, the church continues to spread. Yet there is still opportunity for the church to continue to grow. The majority of the world is not Christian. Whether we look at the people in our own community or people halfway around the world, we can see that God's church has much more opportunity for growth. Jesus led his disciples for three years, teaching them so that one day they could take his church forward.

Today, we still have the mission of learning about God and sharing the good news with others. Just like the church, our faith begins as a tiny speck. Yet when we pray, go to church, study the Bible, and share God's love with others, that seed will grow in us. If God has the power to grow a bountiful physical crop in your fields from a bag of seeds, surely he can do even greater things with a few seeds of faith.

Managing Resources

Luke 6:36–38

[36] "Be merciful, just as your Father is merciful.

[37] "Do not judge, and you will not be judged. Do not condemn, and you will not be condemned. Forgive, and you will be forgiven. [38] Give, and it will be given to you. A good measure, pressed down, shaken together and running over, will be poured into your lap. For with the measure you use, it will be measured to you."

AS FARMERS, much of our success relies on how well we treat our resources. If we take good care of our livestock, they will be healthy and produce. If we neglect them and provide only minimal care, they will produce low-quality products. The same is true for the crops and the land. Well-managed soil produces high-quality crops, but stripping the soil of all nutrients will hurt us down the road. Even machinery will perform better and last longer when well maintained and matched with tasks that are appropriate for the size of the machine.

Agriculture is about building a quality relationship with the people, livestock, land, and other resources we rely on for success. When we provide good care and balance all these resources, we can be successful. Yet when we neglect even one area, our entire farm can suffer. I have met farmers over the years who do not manage their resources well. Their cows barely get milked once a day, the crops get planted in midsummer, and a harvest before Christmas would be unusual. Their resources are not well managed, and as a result they produce low yields.

Jesus instructs us that we too need to manage the resources of people in our lives. We interact with many people: family, strangers, neighbors, and friends. At some point in our lives (and probably many times), we will wrong someone, and are likely to be wronged by someone. When someone upsets us, it is very easy for us to become angry with that person. We wonder how they could be so insensitive or cruel, and forgiveness is the last thing on our mind. But we need to remember that we will mess up at some point too. Chances are that we have done something to the other person at some point in the past. We need forgiveness just as much as this person needs our forgiveness.

As humans, offering forgiveness can be hard. We must put aside pride and humble ourselves to give or ask for forgiveness. We are reminded, though, of the great forgiveness offered by Jesus. No matter how many times we mess up, Jesus will forgive our sins if we come to him with a completely repentant heart. He instructs us that to be repentant, we need to show forgiveness to others. If we cannot offer forgiveness, Jesus cannot do the same for us either. Just as our farm relies on quality input to achieve quality output, our relationship with Christ and receipt of his forgiveness require that we too offer forgiveness, love, and care to others.

It is easy to ask God for help in prayer, and this is certainly a good practice. Yet it is important to examine our lives and look at what we do for others. Do we share God's blessings? Do we share his love? God has blessed you physically, financially, and spiritually. How do you use those resources to give back to him? When we give back to God out of pure happiness for the gifts he gives us, we give a gift that is pleasing to him. Otherwise we are nothing more than ungrateful receivers.

My Shepherd

Psalm 23:1–4

¹The LORD is my shepherd, I lack nothing.
²He makes me lie down in green pastures,
he leads me beside quiet waters,
 ³he refreshes my soul.
He guides me along the right paths
 for his name's sake.
⁴Even though I walk
 through the darkest valley,
I will fear no evil,
 for you are with me;
your rod and your staff,
 they comfort me.

"EVERYTHING IS GOING TO BE OKAY." You have probably heard this phrase shared by a friend at some point in your life. It may have been at a funeral, after a storm that destroyed your crops, during an illness, or at some other time of despair. We face a lot of struggles in life, and with the challenges of farming it sometimes seems like we get more than our fair share of problems. When we are down and out, life can seem hopeless. Yet as Christians we have a comfort that is not available to non-Christians: the power of Jesus.

Psalm 23 is a popular reading at funerals. This psalm, written by David, reminds us of God's strength in our lives. David uses the viewpoint of a sheep to explain God's power. Sheep are viewed by many as helpless animals that need protection. Without Jesus, we too are nothing. David describes God as our shepherd in our lives, and says that we don't require anything. God provides for our needs. Even when we seem to be out of money, food, or daily needs, God provides for us. We might not get the choice or quantity of food that we would like, but God keeps us fed. He provides us with clothes and shelter.

God leads us throughout our lives. He led you to be a farmer. He needs you to produce food and resources for other people. It is because of him that your crops grow and produce, and that you have a harvest. He gives the green pastures, the sunny days, and the rainy nights to let your farm produce. He gives us peace in what we do.

There are also dark days in our lives. Yet, when struggles come, we know he will be by our side. Jesus is there, whether the times are good or bad. As long as we want to keep him by our side, he will be there. When struggles strike, we experience mixed emotions, wondering why this happened to us. We may be scared, not knowing what the future holds. There is no need to fear. Times may not be easy, but God will help us through them.

If you are facing struggles today, ask God to walk with you. Give him your struggles in prayer. Read Psalm 23 again. God has promised to be by your side, and he will help you. We also know that no matter how dark our life may be on earth, a day of glory will one day come. Heaven will be our eternal home. There will be no more suffering there and we will be at God's feast forever. That promise of salvation can be a great comfort, no matter what your struggle may be.

Dirty Jobs

Isaiah 64:6

⁶All of us have become like one who is unclean,
 and all our righteous acts are like filthy rags;
we all shrivel up like a leaf,
 and like the wind our sins sweep us away.

IT IS NOT A SECRET that farming is a dirty job. It seems like no matter what you do, at the end of the day you go home dirty. Usually, on a farm, being dirty is not too much of a problem. There is no one around who expects us to stay clean in our work. However, we have a vegetable farm with an on-farm store. Customers come into our store and expect the cleanliness and fresh appearance of a retail store. Unfortunately, this means that I too am expected to look clean.

I do try hard to look clean around customers. However, when I have just come from picking sweet corn in a wet cornfield, there is only so much I can do. I may quickly replace my muddy shirt and throw on a clean baseball cap, but there is rarely enough time to pull on dry jeans. Considering how I looked fifteen seconds earlier, I feel very clean. I step out front to help a customer, but they may not agree with my sense of cleanliness. The wet pants are very obvious, I have a streak of mud on the back of my arm, I have pollen dust all over anything that is not fresh clothes, and I probably smell of sweat. Despite my efforts to look clean, I am far from clean and can fool no one.

As Christians, we sometimes try to put on our "clean clothes." We work hard to be strong followers of Christ. We serve others, offer a portion of our income back to God, and live each day doing our best to follow him. We know sin has made us dirty, but try our very best to put on clean clothes. However, Isaiah writes that even our cleanest clothes are still covered with filth. We simply do not have the tools or the power to be truly clean.

God knew that man was hopeless on his own. Sin had corrupted his world, and no matter how much people loved God they simply could not be pure on their own. They needed something more. That is why God sent his son, Jesus, to be our savior. Jesus was different in that he did not sin, so his clothes were pure. He was not bogged down by the filth that we wear.

As Christians, we know that one day we can be pure again. We may not have the power to wash away our sins, but Jesus does. He takes our sins for us. When we ask for forgiveness, he washes away that sin forever. It is forgotten, and we are once again pure. When we believe that Jesus is our savior and has the power to wash our sins, we have hope for the future. We know that one day Jesus will wash our sins one final time as we enter heaven. We will be free from sin and pure as we spend eternity in heaven with God and everyone who believes in Jesus.

Sharing the Harvest

Luke 12:15–21

[15]Then he said to them, "Watch out! Be on your guard against all kinds of greed; life does not consist in an abundance of possessions."

[16]And he told them this parable: "The ground of a certain rich man yielded an abundant harvest. [17]He thought to himself, 'What shall I do? I have no place to store my crops.'

[18]"Then he said, 'This is what I'll do. I will tear down my barns and build bigger ones, and there I will store my surplus grain. [19]And I'll say to myself, "You have plenty of grain laid up for many years. Take life easy; eat, drink and be merry."'

[20]"But God said to him, 'You fool! This very night your life will be demanded from you. Then who will get what you have prepared for yourself?'

[21]"This is how it will be with whoever stores up things for themselves but is not rich toward God."

AS FARMERS WE HAVE good years and not-so-good years. Sometimes we are profitable, and sometimes we barely make ends meet. Even though we may do exactly the same work two years in a row, our end result may be different. We have no control over commodity prices, costs can fluctuate, and the quality of the crop can depend on the weather. Disasters can wipe us out, and perfect weather can give us a surprisingly high yield.

What do you do in a good year? What happens when you have a good year that pays well and you end up with more profit than you had hoped for? Do you take a vacation? Do you upgrade your equipment or pay down a mortgage? Do you give an extra portion to God? In today's parable of the rich fool, a farmer had just such a year. The crops yielded well, and he said to himself, "What should I do with such a large crop? I have nowhere to store this abundance, which is more than I can use." The man chose not to give thanks to God, but rather to build more storage so he could relax and be lazy. God did not like the man's plan, and he took the man's life because of his greed.

What is wrong about saving for the future? In and of itself, there is nothing wrong with saving toward our future. Saving some of our money rather than spending all of it is a part of being a good steward of what God gives us. The man in the parable, though, made one major mistake: he forgot about God. He did not offer anything back to him. He had plenty to share, and would still have had leftovers for himself, but he chose to keep it all. Giving back to God is part of what makes us thankful for the things he gives.

How much should we give back to God? Should we follow the biblical model of ten percent of all we have? Is an extra hundred dollars in the offering plate enough after a good year? If we have a lousy year does that mean we do not have to give anything back to God? Your number and how you give it back to God will vary from person to person. The key is to actually make a sacrifice. How do you give an amount to God that will make you stand up and realize that you are giving a significant portion back to God?

A pastor once shared a story about a young student who pledged to tithe ten percent of all he made. Working his minimum-wage job he gave God about ten dollars each week and he felt content. Ten years later he went to the pastor, troubled. He said that he knew he had promised to give ten percent, but that was really hard now. He had recently been promoted to regional manager and was now making $52,000 a year. Now he was giving God over $5,000 a year! How could he afford that? The pastor responded, "I suggest you ask God for your minimum-wage job back so you will not make so much money."

As farmers we do not make a regular income like most of society, and this does require special money management. Yet we always have an opportunity to remember God. When successful years come along, make sure you thank God both in prayer and by giving back his blessings. Set a price point that works for you, and that helps you to feel sacrificial when you give your money to God. If you look at your giving as a line-item number, how important is God in your life? What other financial priorities are coming before him? Let your gifts become a gift of joy and sacrifice, and your gifts will be a true gift of love to God.

Learning to Do, Living to Serve

Matthew 21:28–31

²⁸"What do you think? There was a man who had two sons. He went to the first and said, 'Son, go and work today in the vineyard.'

²⁹" 'I will not,' he answered, but later he changed his mind and went.

³⁰"Then the father went to the other son and said the same thing. He answered, 'I will, sir,' but he did not go.

³¹"Which of the two did what his father wanted?"

"The first," they answered.

Jesus said to them, "Truly I tell you, the tax collectors and the prostitutes are entering the kingdom of God ahead of you."

OUR FARM IS a busy place with lots of work to be done. We do a pretty good job of assigning work roles and dividing up tasks among managers and workers. Yet sometimes we get busy and little jobs slip through the cracks. I know I am guilty far too many times of forgetting to do an important job. I can think of a number of instances when someone asked me to take care of a task. I say that I can complete it, but then I forget or get busy and it does not happen. When I am reminded later, I find that it has already been done. Even though it was my job and I said I would do it, I failed and someone else had to come in and take care of my work.

Do you ever agree to do work and then fail to deliver on your promise? Does someone have to step in and do the work? While the work may get completed without you, who gets the credit? On a farm it often does not matter who does the work, as long as it gets done. A job is just a job that needs completing. If it gets completed, then we are satisfied.

Christianity does not allow us to push our work onto others. In the parable of the two sons, Jesus describes one son who did the work and one who did not. The work gets done in the vineyard, but one son is missing out on the gift. A relationship with Jesus takes work on our part. If we turn our back on him, we are unable to be with him. We cannot simply step into the drugstore and pay to have a relationship with Jesus. We cannot simply take credit for what someone else has done. We need to do the work ourselves. We need to fill our lives with prayer, Bible study, service, and an ever-present connection to God.

Saying that we are Christians does not get us very far. Going to church once a week does not get us to heaven. We need to have a genuine belief in Jesus Christ as our savior. We need to have the desire to serve and obey him. We need to grow daily in the love of Christ. We need to act as a follower of Christ. If we go to church on Sunday but hide our faith the rest of the week, then we are not doing what God wants us to do.

Instead, we need to share Jesus' love daily. We need to do the work God calls each of us to do. Saying is not doing, but doing speaks loudly. Today, ask yourself if you are just *saying* that you love God or if your life *shows* your devotion to God.

Strangers Among Us

Exodus 23:9

[9]"Do not oppress a foreigner; you yourselves know how it feels to be foreigners, because you were foreigners in Egypt."

EXODUS IS AN INTERESTING BOOK. The stories of the plagues in Egypt are followed by the escape to the desert, and the book ends with a number of chapters listing rules for the Israelites to follow. We often skip over these last chapters because we do not extensively study some of the ancient laws or the specifications for how the Israelites were supposed to build the Ark of the Covenant.

Exodus 23:9 is a command from God that is still important to society today even though it is often overlooked. In fact, failure to follow it leads to problems for many today, in almost every country of the world. Even in the United States it is a recurring political issue, yet like most politics, God's commands are not examined when making laws.

God instructs us not to oppress foreigners. That seems easy enough, but what does this have to do with a devotional related to farming? Of the close to one million farm workers estimated by the USDA, an estimated eighty-five percent of them are immigrants. That puts a lot of foreigners on U.S. farms. Certain sectors of agriculture use more immigrant laborers than others, but chances are you or someone you know may employ people whose nationality is not solely American.

I am not here to debate immigration, legal or illegal, or talk about what needs to be done to solve this situation in agriculture. I am not also trying to persuade by taking rough stabs at biblical context to support a specific position on immigration. However, as Christians we do have certain obligations on a more personal level.

God tells us not to oppress a foreigner. This includes a number of things. First, we should not take advantage of immigrants. This means we should pay a fair wage that compensates for equal work performed by nonimmigrants. We should not use inappropriate threats to not pay workers or withhold earned wages. We need to provide safe working conditions and housing that we can be proud of.

We also need to show Christian love. This means we should not make racist comments or put others down because of their race. We need to be understanding of language barriers, and try to offer the help we would want if we had to suddenly move to a foreign country.

Most employers are good people who really do care for their workers, no matter what race they may be. Farm work can sometimes be low-paying hard work. Yet we still have the opportunity to show care and Christian love. When we develop friendships with the people we employ, we have the opportunity to share God's love.

America is viewed by many outsiders as a very Christian country, even though we know this is not true of many people living here. That being said, we are a representation of Christ to our workers. We never know how God may use us to reach out to those around us. You may not know how God plans to use you to share his story with others. Whether he calls you to share him with your fifth-generation neighborhood farmers or a person who has newly arrived from a foreign land, show his love to everyone you encounter.

The Mystery of a Seed

Mark 4:26–29

[26] He also said, "This is what the kingdom of God is like. A man scatters seed on the ground. [27] Night and day, whether he sleeps or gets up, the seed sprouts and grows, though he does not know how. [28] All by itself the soil produces grain—first the stalk, then the head, then the full kernel in the head. [29] As soon as the grain is ripe, he puts the sickle to it, because the harvest has come."

IT CAN BE AMAZING how a seed grows. We drop it in the ground, throw a little soil over it, and there is a good chance it will grow on its own. Certainly we can provide extra tending that will help it grow better and have a higher success rate, but in many cases it would probably grow without our help. In fact, most of nature grows and produces plants without any human help. The power of God to produce living things is amazing.

Most of us do not understand the intricacies and specific science of how a seed grows, but that does not really matter to us. Just as we do not need to know how all the parts in our tractor work or how our computer can perform everything it does in order to use the equipment, we can grow a crop without understanding the power that makes it sprout. The plant grows and produces, makes a fruit, and eventually is ready for a harvest. When the crop is fully ripe, it is cut down and taken to be used.

Our lives and faith are much like that seed. God scatters us on the earth when we are born, and he puts us with loving families that will care for us. Just as a farmer intends for his seeds to grow, God intends for us to grow too. And just as the farmer does not know exactly why the seed grows, we do not know why we grow. How could it be that we come to know God? To an outsider, the stories of the Bible may seem like farfetched tales that only a fool would believe. We may not understand what happened in our life to make us so certain that God is true and alive in us.

In life we do not always put all the right plans into place to allow us to be successful. We make mistakes, cause problems, and get brought down by the struggles of this world. Yet God places important people in our lives. He gives us ministers to help us grow our knowledge, family to encourage our faith, and friends to support us in times of need. We may not always recognize these resources as even being important to us, but God places what we need around us each and every day. He knows the time for his harvest is coming, and he uses these invisible resources to help prepare us for that day.

There is a time coming when we will die and be taken to heaven. Death can be scary for some, but we know that it is just the beginning of something great. Just as the harvest of a crop can lead to production of a wonderful material or food, our time after this life will be great too. Until then, we still have a job to do here on earth.

If you plant a single seed of corn, it will not pollinate well. It needs to be surrounded by many other corn plants. The same is true for Christians. We can grow in faith a little on our own, but we have the opportunity to bless and be blessed by those around us. When we live and work together in God's field, his harvest will only grow more.

Love Your Neighbor?

Matthew 5:43–44

[43]"You have heard that it was said, 'Love your neighbor and hate your enemy.' [44]But I tell you, love your enemies and pray for those who persecute you."

LOVE YOUR NEIGHBOR. My family has always been fortunate enough to get along with our neighbors. Certainly, though we have some neighbors that are friends, others are merely acquaintances, and with some we prefer to keep the conversations fairly short. We have some who would lend us or help with anything, and others we would probably never even ask for a favor, simply because we are not close. Yet my family gets along with our neighbors, and I wouldn't use the word *hate* to describe any of them.

Unfortunately, I have met people who do not have nearly as good a relationship with their neighbors. Sometimes there is an ongoing feud. John's cows keep breaking a fence and getting into Steve's alfalfa. Steve has been known to go around and swipe gas from Roger's fuel tanks at night. Roger is mad because Emily keeps letting sprays drift over his organic fields. Emily is mad because ten years ago John's friends from town shot a deer on her side of the fence. And don't forget about the Johnsons, who have hated everyone in the neighborhood since 1912 for some unknown reason, even though there have been three generations since then. Does this sound familiar? While the examples above may be extreme, your neighborhood probably has its problems.

Who is your enemy? *Enemy* is a strong word, and many of us like to think we do not have any enemies. Or maybe our enemies are unknown distant people such as terrorists or politicians. Yet we all have people in our lives to whom we do not show perfect love. It might be a person who annoys us, or someone who once did something that made us angry. We might have tried to show love before, but they come right back and wrong us again.

Jesus instructs us that, no matter what we do, we need to continue to show love to those around us. Whether they are our enemies or just someone we would rather avoid, it is our job to show Jesus' love. See, we know that we are not perfect. We have messed up before, and we will continue to make mistakes until the day we die. But no matter how many times we mess up, God will still love us. We can turn our backs on him, but he will always continue to show us love and ask us to come back to him.

If someone is difficult for you to get along with, chances are others struggle with that person too. This may be all the more reason why you need to show them love. If no one has made the effort to be kind or has been able to break through this person's shell of difficulty, then he or she may not know what it feels like to have a friend. You have the opportunity to show compassion, and Christ may work in you to take that love even further.

Who Let the Cows Out?

Exodus 23:4–5

⁴"If you come across your enemy's ox or donkey wandering off, be sure to return it. ⁵If you see the donkey of someone who hates you fallen down under its load, do not leave it there; be sure you help them with it."

I CAN SAY WITH absolute certainty that I have never encountered a donkey wandering around my neighborhood. If I did, I would have to wonder why there even is a donkey in my neighborhood! Yet I can think of numerous times when cows have been loose in my neighborhood. Sometimes they were our cows wandering around, and other times they were the neighbor's cows out for a stroll.

It seems like there are always three options when you find a group of cows wandering where they should not . . . which is usually in the middle of the road, at night, in the rain. First, you can simply drive on and ignore them. You may be busy, tired, or simply do not want to be helpful that day. The second option is to stop and help get your neighbor's cows back home. The last option is to claim anything that roams around. Though it would be stealing, you may have the opportunity to lead that animal to your farm. You may run the risk of someone tracking the cow, and with today's technology such as microchips it may be hard to steal an animal. Yet it could be done with a little work.

In Exodus, God was giving the Israelites instructions on how to live their lives. He gave them only one option for wandering animals: return them. While a wandering animal may seem like a daily occurrence or a minor detail, it offers an opportunity to show our Christian love. Obviously, stealing the animal would be dishonest and would break the eighth commandment. However, if we drive by and leave the animal, we are not showing God's love.

As Christians, we have the opportunity to help a friend or stranger when they are in need. If we look at the story of the Good Samaritan, we see a man who was rejected by others three times because they were unwilling to get their hands dirty and help a man who was truly in need. Yet the one who was least likely to help stopped and went above and beyond to care for the man.

If God's people do not help those in need, who will? While his command refers to livestock, it stretches far beyond helping your neighbor with his or her animals. God wants all of us to share his love with others. We have the opportunity to serve those in need in thousands of different ways. Some choose to help those within their church who need a helping hand. Others collect and serve food for the homeless, help the elderly with yard work, or give children a place to learn and grow within their communities. A wide variety of groups works to serve those around the world by building homes, providing medical supplies, or helping clean up from disasters.

There is no lack of service opportunities in this world. We Christians simply need to dedicate our time to them. Working a job 365 days a year can make us feel bogged down and give us an excuse never to volunteer to serve. Yet we all have opportunities. Work with your pastor, church, or community outreach to find an opportunity to help those around you. Even when you are not formally volunteering, look for daily opportunities to serve others. You never know: the neighbor's cows might be out.

Growing Your Fruits

Galatians 5:22–23

[22]But the fruit of the Spirit is love, joy, peace, forbearance, kindness, goodness, faithfulness, [23]gentleness and self-control. Against such things there is no law.

AS A FRUIT AND VEGETABLE FARMER, I can tell you that fruits do not grow on their own. They take lots of care. Fruits and vegetables can be a lot trickier than field crops because they require constant attention throughout their growing life. For example, we plant a new field of strawberries in April. This is done by planting small rootstocks that were carefully grown and raised for this purpose. After planting, we immediately need to start watering the plants. For the rest of the summer, we carefully water and weed the plants. If we do not regularly water, the tender young plants will die. In June, we cut off all the blossoms so that the plants put their efforts into producing more foliage rather than berries. When winter comes, the berries are covered with mulch to protect against spring freezing, and in the spring the mulch is removed. After one season of growing just plants, we can finally harvest for the next three years, but there will still be lots more work ahead.

Strawberries are just one example of the effort needed to produce a piece of fruit. Every fruit is different, whether it grows on plants, bushes, or trees. Most require plenty of effort, but the proper work is what allows them to produce bountifully.

Paul speaks about the fruits of the Spirit in his letter to the Galatians. He lists nine different fruits or attributes. Just as fruit plants need care and effort to produce properly, the fruits of the spirit do not appear overnight. They do not simply appear because we are Christian or because we want to do the right thing. They take effort and practice. As we grow these fruits, there will be times when we make mistakes and exhibit the opposite.

How do these fruits require effort? If we trust God then they should all just happen, right? Let's take a look at joy, for example. Often when people lose a family member, especially a child or spouse, they can become withdrawn. They do not show much joy. It is not because they are necessarily trying to be depressed; they simply do not feel a strong sense of joy. They are unable to see and celebrate the good around them with their loved one gone. Yet they will not be able to simply say, "I am going to start being happy from now on." Instead, it will take careful tending from themselves and help from God and others to move past the lingering grief. With practice, though, there is the hope that joy can return.

All of the fruits do require work. They can seem like simple tasks, but becoming good at any of these skills takes practice. Some of us will catch on faster to certain fruits than others. While we grow, our fruits will have to combat the weeds of evil, such as hatred, sadness, anger, impatience, cruelty, deceit, unfaithfulness, harshness, and a lack of self-control. Satan uses these evils in many ways to try to prevent our growth of the fruits, and if we are not careful they will choke us out. Yet through Jesus we have the power to overcome evil, and he will be our instructor as we develop our fruits.

Growing your fruits will take effort. What fruit or fruits are weakest in your life? What are you going to do to help these fruits grow and be more apparent in your life?

Listening to the Son

Luke 20:9–16

[9]He went on to tell the people this parable: "A man planted a vineyard, rented it to some farmers and went away for a long time. [10]At harvest time he sent a servant to the tenants so they would give him some of the fruit of the vineyard. But the tenants beat him and sent him away empty-handed. [11]He sent another servant, but that one also they beat and treated shamefully and sent away empty-handed. [12]He sent still a third, and they wounded him and threw him out.

[13]"Then the owner of the vineyard said, 'What shall I do? I will send my son, whom I love; perhaps they will respect him.'

[14]"But when the tenants saw him, they talked the matter over. 'This is the heir,' they said. 'Let's kill him, and the inheritance will be ours.' [15]So they threw him out of the vineyard and killed him.

"What then will the owner of the vineyard do to them? [16]He will come and kill those tenants and give the vineyard to others."

When the people heard this, they said, "God forbid!"

I HAVE ALWAYS FOUND the parable of the tenants fascinating. First, I find the symbolism much easier to understand than that of some of the other parables. Second, while Jesus was the one who told this parable, he as the Son of God was correctly predicting his death. The historical context means we can sometimes lose the meaning of some parables, so let's retell the story in modern terms.

An old Iowa farmer had a thousand-acre farm. He was getting up there in years, and decided to take a season off and head to Florida. He rented his land to some neighbors before he left. When fall came, he sent his account-ant to the farm to collect the year's rent. But the renters knew the landowner was not around, so they harassed the accountant and sent him away, point-ing a gun at him and warning him not to come back. They did the work of managing the farm and they were not going to pay any rent. The landowner sent another accountant, one who was taller and more intimidating, but they chased him away too. Finally, he sent his son who lived and farmed a few towns over. If he came as a fellow farmer and as the son of the landowner, surely they would pay their rent. But the evil renters saw an opportunity. This was the farmer's only son. If he was out of the picture, the owner would have no one to leave the farm to after he died except the tenants. So they killed the son and hid his body. Yet the farmer knew what they had done, and he had the evidence to sentence them to life in prison.

God sent many prophets before Jesus to warn the people of their sins. While this sometimes caused a short-term repentance, the people continued to turn away. Many times, though, the prophets were beaten, ridiculed, exiled, or even killed. The people did not want to hear God's message.

God then sent his one and only son. He became a man so that he could relate to the people. He would walk with them and feel their pain. But the leaders of the church did not want to hear what God had to say. They were greedy and wanted all the power for themselves. Jesus was a threat to them, so they decided the easiest solution would be to eliminate him.

I have always thought that killing the son was a dramatic step for the tenants to take. The guy simply came to collect a little rent. He had done nothing wrong, and did not deserve to die. Yet this is exactly what the world did to Jesus. He came with a message and teaching of eternal life, yet the world responded to him as a heretic. They had him killed like a murderer.

The good news is that Jesus' death was a part of God's plan. Because of Jesus, we now have the gift of eternal life. Even though his death was wrong, he accepted it and took our sins upon him. Because of his death we have the gift of life. We know that we can have eternal life forever because of his great gift.

Storms in the Corn

Luke 8:22–25

²²One day Jesus said to his disciples, "Let us go over to the other side of the lake." So they got into a boat and set out. ²³As they sailed, he fell asleep. A squall came down on the lake, so that the boat was being swamped, and they were in great danger.

²⁴The disciples went and woke him, saying, "Master, Master, we're going to drown!"

He got up and rebuked the wind and the raging waters; the storm subsided, and all was calm. ²⁵"Where is your faith?" he asked his disciples.

In fear and amazement they asked one another, "Who is this? He commands even the winds and the water, and they obey him."

I REMEMBER AS A CHILD the excitement whenever a thunderstorm would approach. It was always exciting to see the weather approach from the west. We had a pretty clear view, and we could see the storm move in across the field. As the rain started falling, half a mile away, someone would always yell, "Here it comes!"

Some storms would be strong, some would be windy with a short hard rain, and some would be relatively peaceful. Often we would not know how strong the storm would be until it was almost on top of us. If a wind suddenly pushed in front of it, blowing everything, we knew it would be a bad storm. Sometimes, though, the clouds might look really ugly, but it would not even rain.

As a child, I enjoyed watching the storms. I understood that tornados were bad and could take our house away, but I always dreamed of seeing one off in the distance. Strong winds were fun, and even cleaning up a downed tree after the storm was an adventure for a child. As an adult, I cannot say that I enjoy storms as much. I now understand the destruction they cause to our crops and farm. I have stood only a few feet from windows that have been blown right out of our barn. I have watched tall trees get pulled up by their roots as they tumble down. I saw the wreckage after an auger toppled onto our tractor, and I have had to right the bridge in our corn maze too many times. I have seen neighborhoods flattened by the power of a single tornado.

We face storms throughout our lives. As farmers, we face a number of literal storms that damage our crops, buildings, and farms. Yet we also face other storms, such as broken relationships, financial struggles, illness, and death. These struggles can be frightening. We can feel alone and abandoned, with nowhere to turn. The disciples felt this fear on the lake. They were on deck seeing the great storm, thinking that Jesus was ignoring them in their greatest moment of need. But despite the size of the storm, he was still with them. Even though he appeared silent to the disciples, he was in control.

As we face storms in our lives, we also can feel very alone. We may pray, but sometimes we feel like God is not listening. We know he is there, and wonder why he does not answer more verbally. Rest assured, though, that God does know your needs. He is there to support you, and he is helping you through your struggles. When you take the time to pray, God is working within you so you remember to put your trust in him. He can be a silent protector. We do not always understand why God chooses to work the way he does, but we do know he has a plan. As we go through life we fulfill parts of that plan. It may take years to understand why you experience a certain storm, and sometimes we never learn the reason. Yet we can rest assured that God does know, and he will continue to work in our lives each and every day, now and forevermore.

You Do Not Get Paid What You Deserve

Matthew 20:1–16(NKJV)

[1]"For the kingdom of heaven is like a landowner who went out early in the morning to hire laborers for his vineyard. [2]Now when he had agreed with the laborers for a denarius a day, he sent them into his vineyard. [3]And he went out about the third hour and saw others standing idle in the marketplace, [4]and said to them, 'You also go into the vineyard, and whatever is right I will give you.' So they went. [5]Again he went out about the sixth and the ninth hour, and did likewise. [6]And about the eleventh hour he went out and found others standing idle, and said to them, 'Why have you been standing here idle all day?' [7]They said to him, 'Because no one hired us.' He said to them, 'You also go into the vineyard, and whatever is right you will receive.'

[8]"So when evening had come, the owner of the vineyard said to his steward, 'Call the laborers and give them their wages, beginning with the last to the first.' [9]And when those came who were hired about the eleventh hour, they each received a denarius. [10]But when the first came, they supposed that they would receive more; and they likewise received each a denarius. [11]And when they had received it, they complained against the landowner, [12]saying, 'These last men have worked only one hour, and you made them equal to us who have borne the burden and the heat of the day.' [13]But he answered one of them and said, 'Friend, I am doing you no wrong. Did you not agree with me for a denarius? [14]Take what is yours and go your way. I wish to give to this last man the same as to you. [15]Is it not lawful for me to do what I wish with my own things? Or is your eye evil because I am good?' [16]So the last will be first, and the first last."

DO YOU HAVE EMPLOYEES? How do you think they would react if everyone got paid the same amount of money, even though some worked half as many hours? I know I would feel I was not getting what I deserved.

As part of my work, I sometimes travel to other farms doing contract work. Ahead of time, I set a price with the customer based on how much labor I think the work will entail. When I get to the farm, the farmer is sometimes surprised at how quickly I can do the work. They expect me to be there for a few days, but I am often done in less than a day. Seeing how quickly I am finished, the farmer may start to wonder if I was really worth the price I charged. I explain that, after lots of years of doing the same job, I am very efficient and can do the work in a short period of time. I know all my steps, and can do them quickly. I am also efficient because I did lots of work before arriving at the farm to make sure everything was ready to go. The work is completed exactly as we agreed. If the farmer had tried to do the same job, without my skills and equipment, it would have taken a week or longer. They usually then agree that the price is fair.

As humans, we are used to comparing fairness. Even with a gift, we can be judgmental. A new television might seem like an expensive Christmas present from your parents, until you realize that your sibling got a brand-new car. Though the television might be the most expensive gift your parents ever gave you, you nevertheless feel slighted.

God gives us the ultimate gift of heaven. As Christians, we try to live our lives in a way pleasing to him. We go to church, give part of our income to charity, and show love to others. While we know that heaven is not earned, we feel like we have at least tried to show our appreciation for what God has done. We may have done this for a few years or even for our whole lives. And then someone comes along who has lived a life full of sin, and becomes a Christian right before they die. Think of the soldier on the cross. He lived a horrible life. He did bad things, and serving God probably was not a priority. Yet, only a few hours after professing his faith that Jesus was the Christ, he joined Jesus in heaven.

If you do not yet call yourself a Christian, do not lose hope. God is willing to take you at any point in your life. It does not matter what you have done in the past. He wants to give you his gift anyway. If Jesus was able to accept a man who was crucified on a cross for his sins, then he can surely accept you too. You just have to ask him into your life. Your relationship with him may be an instant change that you will clearly notice. It will take time. But from the instant you ask Jesus in, you will be called one of his. He will continue to be with you every step of the way.

Mountain Movers

Matthew 17:20

[20]"Truly I tell you, if you have faith as small as a mustard seed, you can say to this mountain, 'Move from here to there,' and it will move. Nothing will be impossible for you."

THERE ARE A LOT of big things on a farm. Silos, barns, and sheds are big. Tractors, combines, and dual tires are big. Cows, horses, and cattle are big. But seeds are tiny, and seem insignificant. I can pick up a bag of corn or soybean seed that might have fifty thousand to a hundred thousand seeds in it. The only thing big about that is the quantity of seeds. Yet corn and soybean seeds are giants in comparison to mustard seeds.

This verse from Matthew has always made me wonder about my faith a little bit. I know that my faith is small, but Jesus tells us that with even a small amount of faith we can move a mountain. I do not want to appear overconfident in my faith, and I know my faith still has much room for development. Yet I would like to think that I at least have the same amount of faith as a small mustard seed. A mustard seed cannot be that hard to match in size, can it?

Faith is defined as complete trust in something. So if I have faith, I need to not only be able to fully believe; I need to eliminate any unbelief. The disciples were perfect examples of believing while holding unbelief. They believed that Jesus was the Christ and his teachings. Yet when things went wrong, such as failing to drive out a demon or fighting a deadly storm on the sea, unbelief kicked in. They wanted to believe, yet they were uncertain why the problems were happening. I don't know about you, but I don't think I could remove all unbelief so that if I asked a mountain to move it would.

Humans are skeptics, and this is the root of our unbelief. Even as Christians we question the scriptures from time to time and wonder what God really means. When we face struggles, we wonder why. We pray to God, yet sometimes we do not get the response we want. We wonder why God answered that way. No matter how hard we try, we will always be human with unbelief deep in our hearts.

We may not be perfect in our belief, but this does not mean we can simply choose not to believe in God or his power. Whether or not I believe that the sun will rise tomorrow, it will still rise. I can choose to believe that I do not need to eat to live, but without food I will eventually die. We could choose to not believe in God at all because we feel our faith will never be good enough. Yet our need for God will still be there. Non-Christians have told me that if they do not believe hell exists, how can they go there? I could believe that prison does not exist, since I have never been there, but if I am caught committing a crime I will go there nonetheless.

No matter what you choose, you have to believe in something. If you choose not to believe in God and his power, your belief just lies elsewhere. By choosing God we put our faith in something far more powerful than we can imagine. While our faith may not be perfect, it does not grow without a tiny start. Even if your faith is only the size of an atom, God still gives you the power to do great things.

What Is Your Flavor?

Matthew 7:15–20

[15]"Watch out for false prophets. They come to you in sheep's clothing, but inwardly they are ferocious wolves. [16]By their fruit you will recognize them. Do people pick grapes from thornbushes, or figs from thistles? [17]Likewise, every good tree bears good fruit, but a bad tree bears bad fruit. [18]A good tree cannot bear bad fruit, and a bad tree cannot bear good fruit. [19]Every tree that does not bear good fruit is cut down and thrown into the fire. [20]Thus, by their fruit you will recognize them."

EVERY YEAR OUR seed dealer comes and plants a test plot of sweet corn at our vegetable farm. For those of you who have only ever grown field crops, let me be the first to say that examining a vegetable test plot is much more exciting than a soybean test plot. This is because, in a vegetable test plot, you get to taste all the different varieties of produce. Instead of just looking at the outward appearance or the plant and fruit, you get to taste each one to see how its flavor compares.

Good sweet-corn flavor is important for us because that is why our customers come back. So we take our test plot very seriously. Our seed dealer leads us through the many different rows of varieties, pointing out characteristics such as ear size, height and strength of stalk, and color of husk. We judge the outward appearance, but the true test comes when we taste an ear of corn. I must say we have been disappointed by some very pretty corn. There have been varieties that produce beautiful ears, but when we bite into it the corn tastes awful. We let our eyes do the judging, and we were disappointed by what was actually inside.

The church is also filled with a wide variety of people. Most are great Christians who help us grow in Christ while we help them grow too. Yet Satan has found his way into the church at times and uses the mask of Christianity to do evil. We have all seen news reports of rogue ministers or churches publicly causing harm to others in the name of Christ. These people appear to be devout Christians, but they are far from it. They may even have good intentions, but their work has been guided by the devil, and now they are causing harm to the church.

It can be scary to think that those who are supposed to be leading us can actually be taking us away from Christ. Just like the corn, they can fit in. They can look like the perfect Christian. We follow them because they look nice, act charming, or can preach a powerful message to us. Yet we sense that something is wrong, and as we dig deeper we realize that the sweet flavor we expected is filled with a bitter taste.

How do we avoid being misled? God has already given us all the instructions we need in the Bible. When we study his word, we more fully understand it and can recognize when teachings go against it. We also need to surround ourselves with true Christians so that we can identify what is right. For example, someone who has always bought their sweet corn from the grocery store does not know what really good sweet corn should taste like. They continue to eat store corn thinking it is good. They may even like our failed test-plot varieties because they do not know anything different. However, when they try a really good sweet corn, they instantly recognize the difference.

We need to stay on our guard as Christians to protect against the evil of this world, both outside and inside the church. Continual development of our faith is important so that we fully understand what God looks like in others. When false prophets come our way, we need to stand behind the shield of the true Christ. Sometimes this means we will take the issue head on, and other times we will turn aside, seeking protection. Regardless, keep God close, and you will be protected.

Tomorrow's Forecast: Sunny and Clear

Proverbs 27:1

[1]Do not boast about tomorrow,
 for you do not know what a day may bring.

I CONSIDER MYSELF a fairly private person. I can get along fine with people, but would never want to be a celebrity. I like the feeling of anonymity. Unfortunately, as the person in charge of marketing for our farm, charged with attracting people from our community, I am usually the one who has to talk to the local media. Since I was in high school I have been talking to newspaper reporters, radio hosts, and television cameras. Yet I try to avoid being photographed, and would prefer it if others had the face time.

Beyond my dislike of attention, I also fear what tomorrow will bring. Since we are a farm, we are often asked how our crops will look this year. As farmers promoting our products, we usually report a good upcoming crop. On more than one occasion, I have forecast a wonderful strawberry crop a few days before the season, claiming there will be three good weeks of berries ahead. Then the rain begins.

Rain and strawberries do not mix well when the berries are ripe. Moist conditions can cause the berries to rot and mold quickly. There may be a lot of good berries, but there are also now more imperfect berries than we would like. My forecast of a wonderful berry crop has suddenly punched me in the face.

I do not believe it is wrong to be optimistic about an upcoming season. In fact, I think not keeping a positive outlook can be harmful to a person if they always worry about the worst-case scenario. Still, humility is important. When we brag about our success, our lives can be turned around quickly. As farmers, we know firsthand how quickly things can change. A wonderful upcoming crop can get destroyed in a windstorm. A champion animal can suddenly get sick and die. High commodity prices can plummet without warning.

It is important to keep our pride in check. Both in farming and our daily lives, we do not know what the next day may bring. This is why it is so important to maintain a strong relationship with God. If you suddenly died, would you be prepared to meet Jesus face to face? Or have you been pushing God aside until you have more time to worry about him? The threat of death should not be the only motivation for staying close to God. Tough times may be around the corner, and we will need his support. If we are not developing our relationship with him now, the foundation will not be there when we really need him. Our faith will be lacking and unable to handle our circumstances.

We do not know what tomorrow will bring. Yet we do know that Jesus will be there standing beside us. How will you be involved with Christ today?

Even Jesus Had Break Time

Mark 1:35–38

[35]Very early in the morning, while it was still dark, Jesus got up, left the house and went off to a solitary place, where he prayed. [36]Simon and his companions went to look for him, [37]and when they found him, they exclaimed: "Everyone is looking for you!"

[38]Jesus replied, "Let us go somewhere else—to the nearby villages—so I can preach there also. That is why I have come."

DURING THE FALL our farm sells pumpkins and provides fall entertainment. This is our final selling season of the year, and our family is usually feeling pretty worn out. We have been working long days since early June, and about the only time we take off is a few hours to go to church once a week. We are tired of customers, tired of employees, and physically tired. It's not that we do not enjoy what we do or the people we are around. Without great customers and employees, our jobs would not be fun. Yet even with the best group of people we get to the point where we need a little alone time.

Once in a while, I try to sneak off for a few minutes to catch a short nap or even sit in the break room to eat a snack. Even five minutes would be wonderful. Yet this rarely seems to work. Within a minute or two, I get a call on my radio, my phone rings, or someone comes looking for me because they need my help. Even though I just want a short break, I have work to do. Winter will eventually come, and then I'll be able sit down.

I can understand how Jesus must have felt when he escaped from everyone early one morning. He just wanted to have a little time to pray alone and be with his father. He wanted a short break from the public appearances. I am sure he enjoyed his work and knew of its great importance, but Jesus was still human. He was tired. He needed a quick break. He wanted a few minutes to collect his thoughts without needing to explain everything to his disciples.

Unfortunately, his time of peace and quiet did not last long. The disciples soon woke up and wondered where he had gone. They sent out a search party, not knowing why Jesus would be taking a break. They soon found him, and his moment of silence was over. Yet Jesus did not turn them away. He knew that they were eager to learn, and it was his job to preach to people in the surrounding villages. He had come to earth to be a teacher, and that is what he must go and do. He got up and left because he knew his time on earth was limited. He had work to do before he left.

Our lives can be busy too. We may feel like there are not enough hours in the day. Planting season, harvest season, and winter weather can make our long days seem even longer. We grow weary. Sometimes it is important to sit down for a minute and rest. Jesus had the most important job in history, yet he still found time to relax and reflect. When we step back, we can better see the entire picture. Sometimes this refocus is what we need to keep our priorities straight. Today, take a break and talk to God. Reflecting on him can be a wonderful way to spend time as you relax. And remember: while Jesus may have rested, God is always on call for us.

Stubborn Weeds

Genesis 3:17–19

[17]To Adam he said, "Because you listened to your wife and ate fruit from the tree about which I commanded you, 'You must not eat from it,'

> "Cursed is the ground because of you;
> through painful toil you will eat food from it
> all the days of your life.
> [18]It will produce thorns and thistles for you,
> and you will eat the plants of the field.
> [19]By the sweat of your brow
> you will eat your food
> until you return to the ground,
> since from it you were taken;
> for dust you are
> and to dust you will return."

I BELIEVE THE WORLD would be a much better place without weeds. If I think of the number of hours I have spent dealing with weeds, I might become overwhelmed. Weeds are everywhere. If your only crops are corn and soybeans, I am not sure if you can have a true appreciation for the struggle of fighting weeds. But if you have ever grown crops that require hand management of weeds, you can understand my frustration.

On a produce farm, weeding is much more labor intensive than simply spraying a little herbicide on the field. Machines can be used to cultivate or till between plants, but this is still usually a slow process. Then, using hoes and our hands, we do all the weeding as we move through the fields one row at a time. It is very frustrating to come back a week later and see that a new crop of weeds is already growing quickly. Sometimes it feels like the weeds will never stop and it would be easier to give up and just let them grow. I have given in to this temptation before, but it always ends with the area being overrun by weeds, and with no hope of a harvest.

Why do weeds even exist? Why did God have to create weeds anyway? My least favorite weed, the thistle, seems to have no practical purpose and is nothing but trouble. Why would God create such a troublesome plant? In Genesis 3 we see God throwing Adam and Eve out of the garden. As a result of their sin against God's only rule, their eyes are now opened to the evils and struggles of the world. They will now suffer from pain, death, and God even specifically says weeds. It looks like I was right when I said weeds were evil!

Adam and Eve might have broken one of God's rules thousands of years ago, but why must we suffer for what they have done? We never ate the fruit of the tree of good and evil. Yet as humans, we still sin. No matter how much we try to be perfect, we will always continue to sin. Just as it is impossible for me to eradicate all weeds from my fields, it is also impossible for me to live a perfect life. I make mistakes, tell lies, hurt others, say bad things, and am unfaithful to God every day. We cannot avoid sin.

Sin can feel overwhelming when it bears down on us. Just as I want to sometimes give up on hoeing my weeds, it sometimes feels as if it would be easier to simply accept that we sin and forget trying to live a life pleasing to God. Yet I know if I stop hoeing the weeds my crops will get choked out and have no hope of producing. When we give up on living and asking for forgiveness, we too get choked out, and lose sight of God. Our lives can quickly spiral away from God and into destruction.

Yet God did not leave us to fight our weeds on our own. He sent Jesus to be our savior. He came to wash away our sins and offer forgiveness. In a way, he is our personal Roundup. He does not forgive only the small sins or offer occasional forgiveness. He completely eradicates all of our sins whenever we come to him. He shows us complete forgiveness that we might live our lives without being choked out by our evil. Jesus gives forgiveness for free, but we need to ask for it. If you had a great tool to eliminate the weeds in your field, you would not ignore it. Are you ignoring Jesus?

God's Gardening Tools

1 Corinthians 3:6–9

⁶I planted the seed, Apollos watered it, but God has been making it grow. ⁷So neither the one who plants nor the one who waters is anything, but only God, who makes things grow. ⁸The one who plants and the one who waters have one purpose, and they will each be rewarded according to their own labor. ⁹For we are co-workers in God's service; you are God's field, God's building.

WHY DO YOUR CROPS GROW? You start the year carefully planning for the upcoming season. You scour hundreds of seed varieties to choose the perfect seed. You may look for genetic or modified traits such as disease resistance, stalk quality, water efficiency, fruit size, or a plant's ability to work with synthetic chemicals. You apply preseason fertilizer to provide the best possible nutrients. Then you carefully plant the seed, keeping the rows evenly spaced, the seeds at the proper spacing, and planting the exact amount of seed to provide the best crop at the optimal cost. Next, you monitor for weeds, pests, and disease throughout the season. You take active and proactive steps to manage these ailments. You monitor for water and provide irrigation when needed. Finally, you harvest, transport, store, and sell another successful crop.

It can be easy to gain confidence in our ability to produce a high-quality crop. If we produce a crop above the average of other farmers, we may believe that our close attention to detail is what produces high yields. We imagine we are successful because of what we do. However, we are only part of the picture. Certainly, we need to provide good work to produce a good crop. It would not be logical to plant our fields this year saying that God will produce a bountiful harvest without us ever doing any work. How you manage your resources will affect your harvest.

Paul reminds us, though, that God is ultimately in control of what we produce. Plants grow from a tiny seed into something great. While we can provide great growing conditions, we have no power or control to actually cause a seed to sprout and grow into a fruiting plant. God is the maker of the universe, and he still controls how plants grow. He holds the miracle of creating something great out of something so small. If he decides he does not want something to grow, it will not. On the other hand, he can at times make miracles happen as he helps crops that would seem doomed to die still produce. Despite harsh conditions, sometimes our crops still produce amazingly well.

In his first letter to the Corinthians, Paul was not talking about his new gardening hobby when he spoke of growing seeds. He was speaking about his work for God and his church. Paul recognized that a farmer can plant and care for a seed, but it is ultimately God who makes it grow. The same is true, Paul says, for the church. You may have pastors, teachers, missionaries, and leaders who try to bring people to Christ. Their work is important because without them there are many who would not hear, be encouraged, or know about Jesus. Yet, just like the farmer, they are only the tools. God is ultimately in control.

I am sure you know people who are not Christians. Sometimes we wish that we could simply flip a switch and make them Christians. We have a great opportunity to do God's work by sharing his love with them, encouraging them, and helping them understand God. Yet we are only tools. God knows their needs and will work on them in his timing. It is important that we continue to encourage and help these people, but we also need to remember that we cannot make the seeds grow. We can tend and care for them, but God is the only one with the final power to cause growth. I encourage you to continue to share his love and gospel with others, knowing that you are a tool God uses to accomplish his work.

A Tale of Two Climates

Deuteronomy 11:10–11

[10]The land you are entering to take over is not like the land of Egypt, from which you have come, where you planted your seed and irrigated it by foot as in a vegetable garden. [11]But the land you are crossing the Jordan to take possession of is a land of mountains and valleys that drinks rain from heaven.

SO FAR IN MY LIFE I have had the opportunity to observe agriculture in two areas outside the United States: Costa Rica and Peru. In the area of Peru that I visited, rain was nonexistent. Located in the foothills of the Andes, the region of Lunahuaná gets a total of one inch of rain each year. The mountains block all rain. In fact, some homes have very little for a roof because a waterproof roof is not needed. Yet a raging river flows through the small valley in which Lunahuaná sits, bringing water down from the high mountains. Canals bring water out of the river and into a complex system of irrigation trenches. Water must be carried to fields, buckets of water are thrown in the road daily to keep down the dust, and water for the people must sometimes be taken from the canals.

In Costa Rica, water is a different story. Costa Rica is mostly rainforest, and I do not recall seeing a single irrigation system the entire time I was there. Most of the farmers I met wore rubber boots all day. With many areas receiving between 80 and 150 inches of rain each year, lack of water is not an issue.

Both countries may be somewhat similar in how they farm, but the amount of rain greatly affects how they work. I am sure Peruvians in Lunahuaná do not often get rained out of their work. They essentially have 365 days a year when they can farm. Yet I am sure they spend a large amount of time keeping their irrigation working properly and monitoring water. In Costa Rica, on the other hand, rainouts are common. Stuck tractors are also probably common. Wallowing through mud is just part of life. Yet the farmers in both countries are doing similar work with a similar goal.

When the Israelites left Egypt and headed into the Promised Land, they too were about to experience a completely new type of farming. Egypt was a desert, but the new land would receive water from rain. They would need to adapt to a new form of farming. They would probably have new struggles to deal with, such as too much rain, pests, or disease, but they would adapt with time. In the end, they would still be farmers. They would still need to trust in God to provide for them.

As Christians, God gives us all types of land on which to live our lives. Sometimes we look at people and can see that they have lived a very hard life. Despite ambition, faith, or work ethic, some people just seem to never get the right breaks. Other people are given a little easier life. They have challenges, but they are not as life-changing as the struggles others may face. In either situation, God wants us to live our fullest for him. Regardless of our circumstances, we are still Christians. God is still with us, guiding and leading us, and we are still his followers.

If you feel like you have been given an unfair hand, remember that God is always there beside you. He is with you every step of the way. God knows what you can bear, so be comforted that he trusts that you will handle even the tough circumstances in your life. Be proud to be a follower of Christ, and be comforted to know that one day you will join all other Christians in heaven with Jesus, where we know we will not need to worry about rain.

Waiting for Your Crops to Grow

James 5:7–8

7Be patient, then, brothers and sisters, until the Lord's coming. See how the farmer waits for the land to yield its valuable crop, patiently waiting for the autumn and spring rains. 8You too, be patient and stand firm, because the Lord's coming is near.

IN FARMING, there is always a lot of waiting. Very little happens overnight. If a young animal is born, you need to feed and care for it for years before it finally produces an end product. If you plant seeds, you wait months for a harvest. If you apply a chemical to your fields, you wait days or even weeks for the bugs, weeds, or diseases to die. We are stuck in a constant state of waiting. We cannot give the animal more feed to make it be ready overnight, and a little extra fertilizer will not cut a month off the growing cycle of our crops. We have no other option than to wait patiently.

Most farmers I know do not plant their crops and then sit idly until the harvest is ready. Instead, we find other work to complete. We multitask and make the best use of any time we have. We make preparations so that our equipment will be in good condition and ready to run. We also monitor the growing crop from time to time to help keep it nourished, watered, and protected against things that will harm it.

When Jesus ascended into heaven, many of the early Christians believed that Jesus would return in their lifetimes. They were getting anxious wondering when he would return. Today we still may wonder if Jesus will hold true on his promise. It has been more than two thousand years and he has not come back yet. What is he waiting for? Could he possibly return during our lifetime?

James reminds us to be patient as we wait. Just as we must wait for our crops and livestock to grow, we must also patiently wait for Jesus. Nothing we do can speed his return. He will come when he is ready. However, this should not make our lives come to a halt as we wait. Just as we do not drop all work until our crops reach maturity, we can also continue to work within our Christian life. First, we need to continue to monitor our own faith by feeding, nourishing, and growing it. It is important that we continue to grow in our own faith and not simply be satisfied with its current state. Second, we need to continue with the work around us just as you complete other tasks around the farm. We need to continue to share God's love with others. We need to be missionaries and tell others about Christ. We need to continue be servants to our community in the name of Jesus.

When we plant a seed, it can seem like the day of harvest will never come. Yet we know that in a few short months that seed will have produced a strong plant with many more seeds. It is hard to comprehend that Jesus may return tomorrow, or that he may not return until long after your death. Yet we need to be ready so that when that day comes there is no question that we belong to Christ.

Weathering the Weather

Genesis 8:22
22"As long as the earth endures,
seedtime and harvest,
cold and heat,
summer and winter,
day and night
will never cease."

YESTERDAY MY THERMOMETER read fifty-five degrees Fahrenheit. This temperature would not have seemed out of place if it was not for the fact that it was January 11 in Wisconsin. If you have ever visited Wisconsin in the winter you know that any temperature above freezing in January is celebrated. While every day has not been in the fifties so far this winter, few days have gotten below freezing, and snow has been almost nonexistent.

Yet I am always surprised by how quickly the weather can change. As I sit here this morning, the temperature is down to thirty degrees and quickly dropping. Snowflakes are beginning to fall, and a winter storm warning is in effect, with the chance of more than six inches of snow today. This is certainly a stark difference compared to yesterday's weather. We have enjoyed a mild winter so far, but we knew at some point it would get cold.

As farmers we deal with plenty of less-than-ideal weather. Livestock farmers here in Wisconsin despise the struggles of winter, such as frozen waterlines, cold equipment, and snow-filled pens. Crop farmers constantly struggle with ever-changing weather as they try to plant, harvest, or simply let their crops grow. I cannot think of any year where the weather did not create challenges. We know the challenges will be there, and we accept them when they come.

After Noah left the ark, God made a promise to never destroy the entire earth again by flood. Many know this story from Sunday school, and we are reminded of this promise every time we see a rainbow in the sky. Yet God also made another promise to Noah. He promised that as long as the earth endures, certain cycles will continue. There will always be a time to plant and a time to harvest. We are going to get times of cold weather, and there will also be really hot days. Summer and winter will always exist, even if we live in a mild climate where snow is not a concern. Days will continue to come, and nights will continue to fall. God is promising that there will be good times and poor times in our life. We will experience bad weather, while sometimes winter may seem like it skipped a year. Whatever we face, though, God gives us the promise that he will still be with us.

When Jesus ascended into heaven, he left us with a promise. He told us that one day he will return and take all believers to heaven to be with him there. The gift of heaven is far greater than being protected from floods or knowing that night will fall. Yet these visual reminders tell us that one day Jesus will return to take us to heaven. At that time, this earth will no longer endure. I just hope God chooses tropical weather for heaven rather than winter weather!

Sacrifices of a Farmer

Numbers 11:4–6

[4]The rabble with them began to crave other food, and again the Israelites started wailing and said, "If only we had meat to eat! [5]We remember the fish we ate in Egypt at no cost—also the cucumbers, melons, leeks, onions and garlic. [6]But now we have lost our appetite; we never see anything but this manna!"

FARMING CAN BE an underappreciated occupation. The work is hard and compensation can sometimes be minimal. Farming is not a typical nine-to-five job, and days off are few and far between. The work can be physically demanding, and it can be a dirty and even dangerous job. Farmers deal with working in extreme heat and cold. They can spend an entire season working hard and still lose money if some part of the system causes a loss. Pay can be inconsistent, and for many farm families the final paycheck is so low that some family members must be employed off the farm to help make ends meet.

I had a public-speaking professor in college who did not understand why anyone would want to farm. He did not understand that students could consider farming to be their main hobby, since it was also their occupation. How could people enjoy a job that appeared to be so undesirable to him? Why would someone choose to work more hours for less pay than what he or she could make elsewhere? Sometimes only a fellow farmer can understand why someone loves farming and continues to do so when there are plenty of other opportunities available. We do what we do because we love what we do, and we believe in the work we do.

After God led the Israelites out of slavery in Egypt and safely across the Red Sea, they felt as if they had accomplished a major victory. But soon they started to lack food, and the people began to grumble. When they looked back at Egypt, they remembered there had been plenty of food there. They may have been slaves, but at least they knew that they would eat every day.

They were going to have a long road ahead of them in the desert. While being a slave is not anyone's first choice, it did seem to be better than desert life. Yet God had a plan for the Israelites, and he knew that the final outcome would be much better than the option of staying in slavery. God led Moses and provided manna, and the Israelites eventually came on board and accepted God's plan.

Christians sometimes also question whether the sacrifices of a Christian life are worth it. We commit ourselves to leading God-pleasing lives, giving a portion of our earnings back to God, and giving our time back to him. Certainly we could all find ways to fill our time rather than going to church. We probably have other ways that we could spend our money rather than giving gifts to God. There are numerous vices that we would happily succumb to if we were not followers of Christ. While we do make sacrifices as Christians, we know the rewards are greater even if the world cannot see them. We know that one day we will go to heaven because of the gift Jesus gives to all Christians. Even on this earth we benefit from our relationship with Jesus as we go about our days. The next time you wonder if your sacrifice for Christ is worth the effort, remember the great sacrifice that Jesus made for you.

Assigned Tasks

Genesis 2:15

¹⁵The LORD God took the man and put him in the Garden of Eden to work it and take care of it.

WHAT WOULD YOU DO if Jesus stopped by your house and asked you to make him dinner? Would you tell him that you did not have time? Would you go to the freezer and pull out a frozen dinner? Or would you at least attempt to make some type of home-cooked meal? You might fuss over making the meal because if you made a disappointing meal for your savior you would feel like you did not try hard enough. You have the opportunity to take extra care of Jesus, and just ordering in pizza might give the impression you are lacking potential.

What if God asked you to do a different job? If you are a farmer, you are doing a job that at some point God asked you to do. You may not feel like there was a very strong presence of God telling you to become a farmer, but we know God has a hand in all that we do. The first thing God did after making humans was to put them in the Garden of Eden to care for the land. Even before the fall of humanity, God had his people working and caring for his creation. And even after being kicked out of the garden, Adam was still tasked with caring for the land.

If God tasked Adam with caring for the garden, this must have been important to him. He wanted his people to care for and utilize his creation with care. He provided the plants as food for people, and he expected them to care for it. God tasked the first humans to be farmers, and he still tasks people to be farmers today. Farmers are expected by God to care for his land and to do his work with care and pride. God expects us to treat our land and animals carefully, as a resource that should not be misused. He expects us to produce a fruitful and healthy harvest to feed his people.

Farming should be taken seriously, and we need to do our best to provide a good product. Just as we would not pull out a frozen pizza if tasked by

Jesus to make him a tasty dinner, we should not carelessly raise crops without carefully monitoring our soil, plants, water, and other resources. He has given us a great responsibility to care for his creation.

All Christians are given more tasks than just caring for crops and animals. We are called to love one another, care for each other, build others up, and support others in their daily lives. Jesus asks each of us to do these things in our daily lives, yet often we do not even do them halfheartedly; we simply do not do them at all! When God gives you a task, take it seriously. The God of the universe has asked you to do some specific work, so be eager to do this work for him.

Fences

2 Samuel 22:29–30
[29]You, LORD, are my lamp;
 the LORD turns my darkness into light.
[30]With your help I can advance against a troop;
 with my God I can scale a wall.

IN THE UNITED STATES TODAY, walls are rarely used to replace fences in our fields. In parts of Europe and other areas of the world, though, fields are separated and protected by stone walls—in part because of many years of stones being removed from the fields. Today we use all sorts of fences, including barbed wire, electric, wooden, split rail, plastic, high tension, and woven wire, to name a few. All these fences have advantages and disadvantages depending on how you will be using them.

Fences are important to our farms. They can be used to keep things in, such as our livestock. At the same time they may work to keep things out. A farm needs to keep its valuable livestock contained in one area while protecting them from any outside danger. A fence around a field may keep grazing livestock in that field one day while they graze, and another day that same fence will protect the new growing crop while the livestock graze elsewhere.

We live in a world with a mixture of good and evil. We want to keep the good in as much as we can, but we are continually bombarded with the evil. The good we have can quickly get overrun and destroyed by the evil we face in this world. On our own, we have no way to build a fence between these two problems. Yet the gift of God in our lives is like a wall built up between the good and evil. We are given the Bible, which can serve as a fence to keep evil out and to keep the good in.

The Bible is not a one-click solution, though. Simply being a Christian will not protect us from all evil. In fact, once that fence is built, Satan tries harder and harder to break down that fence and get to us. Sin comes at us furiously, trying to break into our lives. Yet as we build our faith in Christ, we are ever more able to defend against the evil. We know right from wrong, and we gain more power to resist temptation. We pray daily and ask Christ to help us resist the sin and temptation.

Christ can help us fight off the sin and evil to keep them from overrunning the good in our lives. However, the fence he helps build should not allow us to keep all of our good to ourselves. We need to step outside the security of our little fence and face the world. We need to share the good news of Jesus with all those we meet. We need to show the love of Jesus to the entire world. When we go beyond the walls, we can do amazing work for God.

What Do *You* Think?

Mark 8:27–29

²⁷Jesus and his disciples went on to the villages around Caesarea Philippi. On the way he asked them, "Who do people say I am?"

²⁸They replied, "Some say John the Baptist; others say Elijah; and still others, one of the prophets."

²⁹"But what about you?" he asked. "Who do you say I am?"

Peter answered, "You are the Messiah."

WHAT IS THE BEST WAY to make money farming? What is the optimal amount of corn in a feed ratio for swine? How early should you start planting crops each year? Ask these questions to a hundred farmers, and you may get a wide range of answers. While we may raise the same livestock or grow the same crops as all the other farmers in our neighborhood, chances are that we have at least some practices that are different than others. This could be a result of how we were taught, our specialized knowledge, or our abilities and limitations. All our fields or livestock may even look the same when viewed while driving down the road, but rarely is there a consensus in farming on the specifics of a successful farm.

Jesus knew that many people were talking about him, but he also knew that there was not a consensus about who he was. Some people thought he was John the Baptist who had been raised from the dead. Others thought he could be Elijah returning to earth. Others were not completely sure, but thought he could be one of the prophets. They all knew he was someone important, but they did not understand how important he was going to be to them. They recognized him as a great prophet and teacher, but did not see that he was different. Unlike the prophets who had come before, Jesus had come to die on the cross and save the people from their sins.

Today, there is still doubt about who Jesus was and is. Many world religions other than Christianity believe that Jesus did in fact walk on this earth and teach. They believe he was a great prophet who did great things.

Yet their belief about Jesus ends there. While they recognize him as a prophet, they miss that he was God himself coming to the world as man to save all people from their sins. They have their own theories about who Jesus is, but unfortunately these theories are very wrong. In fact, when they leave out the fact that Jesus as God died for our sins, they miss out on the most important fact.

As Christians, we know Jesus can wipe away all our sins so that we are pure in God's sight. We know that, because of our belief in this power, we will one day go to heaven. We also know that simply believing that Jesus walked on this earth will not be enough for us to get to heaven. While there may be a hundred different ways to grow your crops, there is only one Jesus, who requires one belief. All other paths lead us away from heaven. As we go about our lives, we have the opportunity to share God's love with those around us. Most people, Christian or not, know at least a little about Jesus. Yet they may need your help understanding the power of the savior of the world. Help those you meet understand why Jesus was so much more than just a prophet, and why he should be their savior too.

Labor Shortages

Matthew 9:35–38

[35]Jesus went through all the towns and villages, teaching in their synagogues, proclaiming the good news of the kingdom and healing every disease and sickness. [36]When he saw the crowds, he had compassion on them, because they were harassed and helpless, like sheep without a shepherd. [37]Then he said to his disciples, "The harvest is plentiful but the workers are few. [38]Ask the Lord of the harvest, therefore, to send out workers into his harvest field."

IN 2011, THE STATE OF GEORGIA passed a new law to implement a system to verify if workers could legally work in the United States. The goal of the legislation was to put more unemployed Americans to work rather than having those jobs filled by people who did not have legal status to be in the country. Unfortunately, the domestic workers did not fill in the gaps in labor. The fruit and vegetable industry of Georgia was hit hard. Much of that industry relies on hand labor, and many of the migrant workers who did that work did not have legal status.

Although the law would not take effect for a few more years, it immediately had a negative effect on farms that relied on these workers. As much as fifty percent of the migrant workers never stopped in Georgia as they made their way north from Florida. They bypassed the state, leaving farms strapped for labor. When the local labor pool did not provide the workers needed to complete the work, thirty to forty percent of some crops sat in the field without being harvested because there were not enough laborers to do the work. There was plenty of good produce lying in the field just waiting to be picked, but without someone to come and carry it away there was no hope for it.

Jesus also experienced the frustration of a shortage of workers as he toured the countryside preaching and teaching. Crowds followed him wherever he went, and he had compassion on them. Yet at the end of the day he would pack up and go on to the next town. Jesus knew that he needed leaders in the local areas to continue his work. He saw the great crowds of people who needed his help, but there simply were not enough workers able or willing to accompany him on his journey and tell his good news.

Jesus knew, though, that his work was still building. He was training his disciples daily. They may not have understood at the time, but they would one day become the leaders of God's church and would become the next teachers to go out and instruct God's people. They too would eventually train new leaders who could serve in their local communities.

The world today still needs workers. Billions of people on this planet do not know Christ and have not accepted him as their savior. We still need to carry on the work of teaching others. We do not need to be a pastor or ministry leader to do this work. God has given each of us an understanding of his word. As we continue to learn about his blessings, we continue to be able to share his love. The workers are still few today. Yet, unlike the field workers in Georgia who simply harvest a seasonal crop, when we work in God's fields we grow the workforce whenever we share God's love. Imagine the potential if we all told just one new person about what God has done for us.

A Bad Time to Farm

Exodus 10:13–15

[13]So Moses stretched out his staff over Egypt, and the LORD made an east wind blow across the land all that day and all that night. By morning the wind had brought the locusts; [14]they invaded all Egypt and settled down in every area of the country in great numbers. Never before had there been such a plague of locusts, nor will there ever be again. [15]They covered all the ground until it was black. They devoured all that was left after the hail—everything growing in the fields and the fruit on the trees. Nothing green remained on tree or plant in all the land of Egypt.

MOSES ASKED PHARAOH to let the Israelites go, but time after time he refused. As God sent the ten plagues on the Egyptians, we see God's ultimate power affecting the Egyptians. Some plagues affected their resources, such as the plague of blood, which took away their source of water. Other plagues, such as lice and boils, affected their bodies. Still others affected their agricultural enterprises. The plague of the livestock struck dead every animal belonging to the Egyptians. Later, the plague of hail struck and destroyed the barley and flax because they were near maturity. However, the wheat was smaller and survived the hail. Not long after, though, the plague of locusts destroyed whatever crops were still living. The land and everything growing on it was devastated.

I have experienced some bad years as a farmer, but I cannot imagine the destruction that the Egyptians faced. After they had experienced a number of bad plagues, all their livestock suddenly died. The Bible does not say some; it says *all* livestock. Now, I know that seeds can be saved from year to year to grow crops, but if your entire herd of livestock dies your breeding program is finished. On top of that, hail destroyed two main crops, and it was so severe it even killed people and probably did structural damage. And to top it all off, a swarm of locusts moved in and destroyed what few crops they had left. At this point, their farms were worthless.

The economic impact of the plagues must have been horrible on the Egyptians long after the Israelites left. In addition to losing their labor force, the plagues caused massive destruction that must have been felt for many years to come. Can you imagine being an average Egyptian watching all this destruction happen? I think I probably would have been quite angry with Pharaoh. Why wouldn't he let the Israelites leave? Certainly they were very valuable to Egypt, but the cost of destruction that continued to fall far outweighed the economic benefit of free labor. Slaves would be worthless if all of Egypt was destroyed. All Pharaoh needed to do was turn his heart toward God.

How many times have we disobeyed God? How many times does he need to remind us before we do right? God has given us clear rules to follow, but sometimes we simply choose to continue to ignore him, even though he provides gentle reminders. Why do we choose to ignore him? Is it that we are too stubborn to change, or maybe we keep missing our obvious faults? Yet we do have free will. It is up to us to make the right choice to do good. Sometimes we may need to ask God for help, but we do have the opportunity to do right. When we mess up, we need to ask God for forgiveness. We know that we will not always be perfect. Only Jesus was perfect. We do know, however, that Jesus shares his love with us, and he offers free forgiveness when we repent, whether we continue to sin ten times or a thousand times.

Dividing the Land

Genesis 13:8–11

⁸So Abram said to Lot, "Let's not have any quarreling between you and me, or between your herders and mine, for we are close relatives. ⁹Is not the whole land before you? Let's part company. If you go to the left, I'll go to the right; if you go to the right, I'll go to the left."

¹⁰Lot looked around and saw that the whole plain of the Jordan toward Zoar was well watered, like the garden of the LORD, like the land of Egypt. (This was before the LORD destroyed Sodom and Gomorrah.) ¹¹So Lot chose for himself the whole plain of the Jordan and set out toward the east.

ABRAM AND LOT, two relatives with very successful herds, one day came to the realization that fighting over the land would not bring either of them more success. So they made an agreement that they needed to split the land so that each man could successfully raise his herds. The land was divided into two natural areas. The first area was along the Jordan River and was very fertile. It was so nice that it was compared to the Lord's Garden. The other land was not as fabulous. It would allow him to make a living, but it certainly was not described as the Lord's Garden.

Abram had a choice. He could negotiate a deal with Lot to divide the land fairly, or they could try to divide the fertile and unfertile land so they got half of each. Because that would not have been very practical, Abram stepped forward and let Lot choose whichever piece of land he wanted. Lot chose the prime land, and they went their separate ways. Yet God called Abram and told him that he would be blessed and that his descendants would one day cover and rule his entire land.

Land disputes can be all too common when wills fall to children and heirs try to divide up the land in an inheritance. This can be even more troublesome for farm families, as there is typically quite a bit of land at stake. Most farms have good land and poor land, and deciding who gets what can be troublesome. No one wants the poor land, and with so much value at stake it can be hard to willingly give up good to take the poor.

When God led me to Peru on a mission trip, I learned about how land was passed from generation to generation in the area I visited. Fields were inherently small to begin with, due to the topography, irrigation systems, and methods for caring for the fields. A field larger than an acre was uncommon. As we walked through a field, a young farmer told me that his parents owned three short rows of fruit trees in a small grove. He explained that the grove was owned by about five families. When a parent dies, it is not uncommon for each field to be divided among each of the parent's children. This way each child gets a part of each crop and land rather than one child getting only a peach field while another gets only grapes. Consequently, some fields had become so small that they might only contain a few plants.

As children, we are taught to be polite and let others take the bigger piece of cake, go through the serving line first, and take the last cookie. Sometimes I think we forget this as we become adults. We cut people off on the road, we borrow from others without ever giving back, and we become impatient when a store clerk cannot serve us immediately. Jesus tells us to put others first, and yet sometimes we forget to do that even in the simplest actions. We would rather make sure that we get our fair, equal cut rather than just giving the extra amount.

Jesus made a sacrifice far greater than Abram's. When he went to the cross, he died for all of our sins. We should have paid the price of great suffering, hell, and eternal bitterness. Yet Jesus experienced the most excruciating pain so that we would not be condemned to hell. He made a wonderful sacrifice for us that we might one day join him in heaven.

Unproductive Fruit

Luke 13:6–9

⁶Then he told this parable: "A man had a fig tree growing in his vineyard, and he went to look for fruit on it but did not find any. ⁷So he said to the man who took care of the vineyard, 'For three years now I've been coming to look for fruit on this fig tree and haven't found any. Cut it down! Why should it use up the soil?'

⁸" 'Sir,' the man replied, 'leave it alone for one more year, and I'll dig around it and fertilize it. ⁹If it bears fruit next year, fine! If not, then cut it down.' "

I REALLY DO NOT enjoy eating vegetables. It is not that I will not eat them, but there are few vegetables that I look at and feel excited about putting in my mouth. I eat them out of obligation, not enjoyment. I know this is strange, since I make my living from growing and selling vegetables, but I always say I do not have to worry about eating all the profits when it comes to vegetables. However, fruit is a different story—I love fruit! Of all fruits, strawberries are probably my favorite. And, lucky for me, we grow strawberries.

Strawberries are different from most of our crops in Wisconsin. They are a perennial crop, so with the right care we can pick them year after year. When we plant strawberries, they are just tiny plants that look almost dead. They are spaced about a foot apart, and the field looks very sparse. Strawberries grow new plants using runners, and in time those few plants fill the field with thick rows. To encourage these new plants to put their effort into growing more plants rather than actual strawberries, the first year we cut off the blossoms. Unfortunately, no blossoms means no berries. As excited as I might be about eating those soon-to-be strawberries, I have to cut all the blossoms off the plant. I must say that this is disappointing for me. Yet I know that my patience will produce a much better crop our second year, when lots more plants fill the rows.

Jesus told a parable about an unproductive fig tree. The owner wanted to cut it down, but the gardener asked to give it one more year of care first. He believed that, with extra fertilizer and patience, he could make it produce. He just wanted to have a little more time.

Thankfully, Jesus is also patient with us. Sometimes we may stray from God. He has given us a plethora of gifts, but we still reject him. He could say that he is done with us and that we can try to fend for ourselves. Yet this is not how God works. Instead, he is like the gardener who wants to give us time and extra love so that we produce. He believes we will come back to him. Just as he is described as a shepherd looking for a lost sheep, he wants to put his full care into anyone who needs help bearing fruit.

God knows that we are not perfect. While he does not like it, he knows that we will sin from time to time. We may feel that we have sinned too greatly or too many times, but God is always willing to give us his forgiveness. He is there to love and care for us each and every day. When we stray, he puts the people in our lives who we need to help fertilize and grow us. He gives us a path back to him. Yet it is still ultimately our decision. We have the choice to follow the path toward Jesus or continue to stay away. We know that his path will not always be easy, but we know the end result is always worth any difficulty we may face. If you feel as if you have become separated from God, please ask him to bring you back. His answer will always be yes.

You Produce What You Plant

Luke 6:43–45

[43]"No good tree bears bad fruit, nor does a bad tree bear good fruit. [44]Each tree is recognized by its own fruit. People do not pick figs from thornbushes, or grapes from briers. [45]A good man brings good things out of the good stored up in his heart, and an evil man brings evil things out of the evil stored up in his heart. For the mouth speaks what the heart is full of."

HAVE YOU EVER TRIED raising a completely new crop on your farm? This can sometimes be a difficult process. You may be unfamiliar with planting techniques, necessary soil treatment, and common pests for that crop. You may not yet fully understand proper handling and how to store the crop. When it comes to selling your crop, it may be harder than simply hauling it to your local grain elevator.

The first year we planted muskmelon and watermelon on our farm, it was a challenge. My brother is a far greater expert at production than myself, so he spent a lot of time researching everything we needed to do. We even planted small trial plots for two years first to better understand the melons. We bought specialized equipment, including a mulch layer and transplanter. Finally, the day came to plant. Our first year went fairly well, and we certainly learned lots along the way. We learned that if your plastic is not completely buried, a fifty-miles-per-hour wind will blow it all away. We learned about the pests that would attack the melons and the importance of bees for pollination. Our preparation had helped, but we knew we would continue to learn. Yet if my brother had done no research and simply tried to plant melon seeds in the ground the same way we plant corn, we would have had little success.

As farmers, we excel in what we do daily. When we follow the same tasks day after day for many years, our highly refined skills become second nature. We do these jobs without even thinking. In Luke 6, Jesus tells us that the way we live our lives also becomes natural for humans. He tells us that good trees produce good fruit and bad trees produce bad fruit. What does this mean? I know that if my strawberry fields have old, rundown plants, they will not produce large, tasty strawberries. As Christians, we know that when we live our lives daily in Christ, God's love will show through us.

If we are following Christ, his love should be evident in our daily lives. His love should be apparent in our actions. Likewise, when someone is not a follower of Jesus we should not be surprised when they lie, cheat, or do evil against us. This is not to say that all non-Christians are bad people; they simply do not have the incentive and guidance of Christ that they need in order to be good people. They do not have Christ to follow as a role model. Just as a farmer with a new crop does not yet know the practices to being successful, a non-Christian does not have the Bible as a guidebook in their lives.

Likewise, God expects us as Christians to show his love and do good. When we sin, we are going against what God expects us to be as Christians. We will not magically be perfect starting the day we are baptized, and we will still be far from perfect when we die. I still make mistakes with crops I have been growing for years. Yet when we work at continuing to grow our relationship with Christ, our physical actions will show improvement too. Christ's love does show in our lives. Are you displaying it correctly?

Rain: Blessing and Curse

Zechariah 10:1

[1]Ask the LORD for rain in the springtime;
it is the LORD who sends the thunderstorms.
He gives showers of rain to all people,
and plants of the field to everyone.

DO YOU SAY A PRAYER before your season begins each year? How about a prayer of thanks after your harvest? When your crops need rain do you say a prayer to God, or do you joke that we should do a rain dance? Prayer is important to Christians because it is our way of communicating with God. It is a great gift to be able to talk to God in such a direct way.

Throughout the Bible, rain and drought are recurring themes. Rain can be a blessing, and it can be a curse. God used a flood to destroy the entire earth. He spared his entire creation on a single boat. The lack of rain is also prevalent. There are numerous instances of the need for rain throughout the Bible, including the drought that brought Jacob's twelve sons to Egypt in Genesis and the drought that led to the Baal showdown on Mount Carmel.

Throughout scripture, rain and drought are used repeatedly to punish people for their sins. Rain, when given at the right time, is also considered to be a blessing. When we look at God's promised land, we see land that was full of flowing streams and rain that did not require the irrigation that had been used in Egypt. At still other times, God provided rain independent of the actions of people. In the case of Joseph becoming Pharaoh's assistant in Egypt, the rain was not really a punishment. It was simply a necessary part of God's plan to bring Israel to Egypt. It was the early part of a long story of building trust with his people before he would one day lead them out of Egypt back to their homeland.

Water is vital in sustaining life, which includes our bodies, our crops, and our livestock. Yet we are told in the New Testament that Jesus is the living water. If we drink a glass of ordinary water today, we will be thirsty tomorrow. The same is true of Jesus. We need him today, and we will still need him tomorrow. Yet he is able to fulfill so much more than just a daily thirst. He is able to give us a relationship that will last for eternity. When the last day comes, he will take us home to heaven. Until that time, we do have the gift of prayer to continually be with him. We continually build our trust in him when we pray for rain, and we trust that he will be in control. We grow in him when we thank him for the gifts he provides. If someone provided a miracle fertilizer for free that improved your crops by twenty percent, you would probably be very grateful. God gives us all the blessings our crops need, but we so often forget to give thanks to him for helping them grow. We might not always have a perfect crop, and some years our crops may all die. Yet we know that our life as farmers is only temporary. God does not promise that every crop on earth will be perfect, but he does promise that heaven will be a wonderful place.

Feeding God's Hungry

Leviticus 19:10

[10]Do not go over your vineyard a second time or pick up the grapes that have fallen. Leave them for the poor and the foreigner. I am the LORD your God.

FARMERS HAVE BORNE the responsibility of feeding mankind since God made Adam and Eve. Through God's blessings they have produced crops, livestock, and byproducts. They have fed themselves, their families, and those willing to buy their products. God has also continually given farmers one more command that is seen numerous times in scripture: to provide food to the poor.

In Leviticus 19, God does not command the Israelites to give every last penny to the poor. While this certainly would be a huge step of faith for any believer, God provides other opportunities. When we give a portion of what we have on a regular basis, we keep God at the center of our lives. He is a part of our constant thoughts, and he uses our gifts to strengthen our relationship with him.

God instructed the Israelite farmers to only harvest their fields once. Certainly, they would pick the majority of the harvest on the first pass. Rather than picking a second time, though, he instructed them to leave their remaining crop in the field to be harvested by the poor. This was certainly good crop that could have made money for the farmer. By leaving it, they were providing an offering to God that would be distributed to those in need.

Today there are many companies, both small and large, that donate second-quality products to food banks. Products may get donated for a variety of reasons, such as expiration, damaged containers, or overstocking. These businesses have unsalable product, but they choose to donate it rather than simply sending it to the landfill. While it may not be their first fruits, they understand that it is better to give than to be wasteful.

Most of our crops today are harvested with mechanical harvesters, which results in very little excess grain. Chances are that, even if you left a portion of your harvest in the field, the poor in your community would not know how to use a stalk of soybeans or wheat. Some farms, such as those raising produce, may have the opportunity to donate raw products, but commodity farmers do not usually have this option. Instead, they have other opportunities.

There is always an opportunity to give money or food donations to help others. We can follow the idea to give our seconds by saving our pocket change to give to those in need. We can also help with our hands by providing assistance in preparing food for the needy. God also leaves us with other opportunities, such as volunteering to help with a community garden or a cooking school where our expertise can help educate others about growing or preparing food.

God does not instruct us to simply put an offering in the plate every Sunday. Our local churches need our financial support to continue their mission, but God also instructs us to serve those in need. Whether we give our time, money, or our hearts, we are serving God. This command extends to all people, not just farmers. Sometimes, engrossed in our work, we forget about all that we can do to serve others. Take a moment today and evaluate what you can do to give back to God.

You Are God's Farmer

Esther 4:13–14

[13]"Do not think that because you are in the king's house you alone of all the Jews will escape. [14]For if you remain silent at this time, relief and deliverance for the Jews will arise from another place, but you and your father's family will perish. And who knows but that you have come to your royal position for such a time as this?"

THIS DEVOTIONAL BOOK is coming to a close. In the previous ninety-nine devotions, we have studied God's role in our lives as farmers. We have read stories of farmers who were blessed by God, and farmers who struggled when God allowed less than ideal situations to occur. We have read how the role of the farmer is important to society even if it is not the most spiritual profession.

I chose the reading from Esther to close this book because it is one of my favorite readings in the Bible, even though it is almost meaningless when taken out of context. Esther is a short book and an easy read, and I encourage you to take half an hour and read it. To give a one-sentence background: Esther is a Jew who became queen during a time when there was a plot to kill all the Jews, but she was afraid to interfere to save the Jews for fear of her own life. My favorite part of these verses is spoken by her cousin Mordecai as he begs her to try to save the Jews: "And who knows but that you have come to your royal position for such a time as this?"

When you close this book, you will still be a farmer. Chances are you do not interact with lots of people on a daily basis, and your opportunities to witness in your work may be somewhat limited. Certainly, someone such as a pastor is naturally more likely to encounter and have the opportunity to share about God on a daily basis. Yet this does not mean that God does not have plans to use your position as a farmer to do spiritual work beyond the important physical work you do. This spiritual work may be occasional, or it may be just one significant event at one point in your many years of farming.

Yet God has put you in a very important position, even if you do not yet know its importance.

Esther became queen and probably thought very little about why God had chosen her to fill that role. Yet he had a plan. She became queen for "such a time as this." God put you in your position. He has trained you in his word, and he has helped you learn to trust him. A time may be coming when you will need to lean on everything that God has taught you. What you do may be as a direct result of the fact that you are a farmer. You may interact with another farmer who needs to hear about God. You may save the life of someone who is injured, and the only reason you were there was because you were chasing a cow that got out. You may be called upon to talk to someone about their struggles—not because you are a great minister but because they trust you as being an average person like them. You may be a role model for a young child who wants to do everything just like you.

I do not know what your "such a time as this" will be. Only God does. That time may come and pass you and even you might not realize the significance of it. I grew up in a Christian family, went to a Christian school, and have lived with a strong presence of God in my life. When I was about twenty-one, I was traveling the country one summer cutting corn mazes for farms. Before I left one farm, I had a casual conversation with the farmer, Rick. Rick was a nice guy who loved to talk, and he was always very accommodating and kind. As I was about to leave, he quickly ran into his house and came back with a small devotional book. It was one of those disposal devotional books in which each devotion is written for a specific day over a few months and comes as a subscription. Now, Rick and I had barely even mentioned our faith to each other, but we both knew that the other was a Christian. Yet, as we parted, Rick had decided for some reason that I needed a devotional book while I was on the road. I took the book to be polite, but I really did not intend to read it. I was not someone who read devotions much. Through the rest of that trip, though, I seemed to have more than the usual number of mechanical problems. As I was sitting and waiting at one farm for a repair part to arrive, I decided to open that book and read through a devotion. From that moment, God has reminded me of the importance of staying in his word. He inspired me about our importance as farmers to rely on him.

I will admit that I have not always been as faithful about reading a daily devotion as I would like. I have missed church from time to time, and I probably should be in a better habit of going to Bible studies. Yet, despite my sin, I know that God loves me. That little book from Rick was not a life-changing event, at least not that I know of. Rick has probably not thought about that moment since I left his farm, but God has continued to use that moment for me. He used it to encourage me to stay in his word. He used that moment to plant the seed in my mind to write this book. It took a few years before that process even began, but the seed was planted at that time.

If Rick had been a pastor instead of a farmer, chances are I would have never met him. I may not have ever opened that book if it was given to me by a pastor. Yet God put Rick there in my life for just such a time as that. It was a fairly small moment, and I would probably still be a Christian today if that moment had not happened. Yet you might not be reading this book, someone who reads this book may not take some kind of action, and ultimately someone may not learn about the love of Jesus and the gift of heaven. I cannot begin to fathom the far reaches of the power God provides through little actions.

God is going to use your position as a farmer for great things. Continue to trust in God knowing that he has a plan. He makes things work for his glory. To God, you are much more than just a farmer; you are his worker and child. May he bless your work, whether it involves tilling his soil on earth or tilling his eternal soil.

To God be the glory forever and ever,

Amen.

Acknowledgments

Thanks ...

... to my parents for your love and support, whether it be in farming or faith

... to my family for putting up with me all these years

... to my wife for bringing so much joy into my life and always listening to my crazy ideas

... to Keith, my editor, for once again making my writing so much stronger while also providing your Christian background to help guide my rambling, unlike other editors would have done

... to God for everything I have. As I read through these devotions I wrote months ago, I realize these words are not mine but inspiration from you. Thank you for the good ones, and please forgive any human mistakes.

About the Author

SCOTT SKELLY was born on a farm in southern Wisconsin and has not stopped farming since. When he was twelve years old the family farm converted from dairy and cash crops to vegetable production and a farm market. Through the years, Scott has worked to grow Skelly's Farm Market. With his wife Laura, Scott runs Corn Mazes America to help other farms become successful with new enterprises.

Made in the USA
San Bernardino, CA
09 September 2014